The 21 Laws of Influence

Published by Indaba Press
18 Ridgewood Road, Suite 201
Malvern, PA 19355

ISBN: 1-58570-072-X

Printed in the United States of America

Distributed in the United States by Midpoint Trade Books

For general information contact:

Indaba Training Specialists, Inc.
18 Ridgewood Road
Malvern, PA 19355
www.indaba1.com

T (610) 993-8047
F (610) 993-8721
www.21Laws.com

Hellen Davis has mastered the science of influence and shares her techniques in *The 21 Laws of Influence*. The great thing about her book is you have the option to reading one law, which alone will increase your power to influence, or all 21 to become a master influencer. Of all the personal and professional growth books I've studied over the years, this is a must read.

Shad Helmstetter, Ph.D.   Gulf Breeze, FL
Author of "Who Are You Really And What Do You Want?"

Leading people and satisfying stakeholders is a skill that depends on your influencing abilities. *The 21 Laws of Influence* clearly defines strategies so that you can persuade people to go along with your plans.

James Torgerson   President & CEO
Midwest ISO   Indianapolis, IN

I don't know how you would possibly reach your full potential without understanding *The 21 Laws of Influence*. If you want to make more money, get more clients, motivate employees and have better relationships with friends and family members, you have to know the laws!

Randy Schuster   Senior Advisor
Centra Financial   Rochester, NY

Whether you are dealing with employee issues, handling client negotiations, or explaining corporate goals to your partner, your influencing skills are at work. If you want to achieve your goals with the least amount of resistance, study *The 21 Laws of Influence*.

Will Schwartz   Founder
Intech Construction   Philadelphia, PA

Practitioners of influence have been given a new, comprehensive training manual. *The 21 Laws of Influence* outlined in this book will fascinate any reader interested in gaining influence over others or defending against other people's influence.

Charles P. Garcia   President and CEO
Sterling Investments   Boca Raton, Fl
Author, "Yes, You Can Succeed"

Hellen Davis is a master at influencing people. This book will show you how to persuade others in an effective and efficient manner. What does that equate to? It will help you make more money, faster and easier, than you ever dreamed possible!

Rick Frishman   President
Planned TV Arts   NYC, NY
Co-Author, Guerrilla Publicity

You have to know yourself and what your influencing strengths are, if you think that you can do better or want to make a bigger impact with people, read *The 21 Laws of Influence*.

Stu Zimmerman   President & CEO
Inner Securities, Inc.   Napa Valley, CA

Dedicated to Jack, Jazmin, and Justin, (the Three J's), for all your laughter and encouragement.

We have a great life!

With special thanks to Kate Halligan for her patience during this project. Thank you especially for listening as the ideas for this book started to take shape. Your insight was inspiring and your assistance was invaluable! Thank you Nanci Mueller and Allison Benford (and as always, Jack!) for your eagle eyes and suggestions; and for the constant editing as this book evolved.

I also have to mention Mark Steisel, my editor. With his guidance and help, this book came alive!

For the purposes of confidentiality, I have changed most of the names that appear in this book. I am exceptionally fortunate to interact with some of the best minds in the business world and wish there were some way that I could acknowledge their contributions while protecting their confidentiality. So, to the many people who contributed to this book, please understand why you remain anonymous. Thank you for allowing me to share your insights, lessons, and knowledge, and for your permission to pass that knowledge along to others.

ABOUT THIS BOOK

This book is a collection of white papers written by master influencer and sales authority, Hellen Davis, the founder and CEO of Indaba Training Specialists, Inc. It is a practical book intended to show you how 21 basic laws control influence. After reading this book, you will have a greater understanding of how to exert influence over other people's decisions and how to detect when others are trying to influence you.

All of the information in this book is based on actual, field-tested, real-life experiences, not merely theoretical ideas. It is jam-packed with case studies taken from Hellen's vast experience working with a wide range of clients, many of which are major corporations. It also includes anecdotes, examples, insights, quotes and comments that will improve your understanding of influence.

The principal audience for this book is people who, in order to succeed, must be able to influence, persuade, and communicate convincingly. It has been written and designed primarily for leaders and those who aspire to lead, no matter what their rank. This approach also helps us avoid the risk that certain readers will erroneously translate messages that were not written for them.

This is not so much a book to be read, as it is a practical volume to be used. You do not have to read it from cover to cover or in any particular order for you to understand the peak-performance concepts that control influence, language, and communication. This compilation has been designed to allow readers to examine each section as an individual module and to apply the concepts of that unit to their own particular situations.

We strongly believe that if you open this book to any of the chapters, you will find ideas and insights that will enhance your ability to effectively influence, persuade, and communicate with others.

Table of Contents

Why is it so critical to understand *The 21 Laws of Influence*? It's because the *21 Laws* are based on typical behavior patterns that people consistently follow. From childhood, we have been conditioned to act in a particular manner when confronted with certain sets of circumstances. When problems arise, we instinctively turn to solutions that have worked well for us in the past and we feel comfortable, even confident, with them. Before we know it, societal norms have programmed us to think and behave in repetitive and predictable patterns. These patterns form the basis for the decisions we make, the actions we take, and how well we succeed.

Understanding *The 21 Laws of Influence* will teach you how most people will act during the influencing process. The laws themselves are neither good nor evil, they simply explain how society has indoctrinated us to react and respond. Many of our actions, reactions, responses, and mannerisms are governed by what society considers are the boundaries of acceptable behavior. In other words, we are creatures of habit.

Influence is based on the behavior of the influencer and the actions of the target, the person who the influencer is trying to persuade. Strategy and communication are at the core of influence. The more an influencer is able to tie their influencing strategy to their goals and objectives, the better they will succeed.

In order to become a 'Master of Influence', it's essential to understand the laws that govern the influencing process. *The 21 Laws of Influence* will teach you how to predict most peoples' responses, which will greatly enhance your ability to influence them. It will also help you recognize when any of the *21 Laws of Influence* are in play and could be used against you. Then, you can ask, "Am I basing my decisions on societal habits, on my goals, or both?" This may just give you the edge you need to succeed.

This book was written to illustrate how to influence others in a positive manner: clients, peers, customers, prospects, employees, family members, and upper-level management. I wrote it specifically for anyone who wants to better understand the process of persuasion and influence and how it can work for or against you (if you aren't aware of it!).

Study *The 21 Laws of Influence* and then apply your newfound knowledge to your personal and professional life. Take my advice – mold the lessons and concepts of each law to your individual style. Never try to adopt an influencing technique that does not work with your personal communication, management, or sales style. If you do, it will be a disaster! Your targets will sense incongruence; they will recognize that things don't fit, don't add up, or are amiss. When incongruency exists, trust deteriorates; and you will fail.

Apply the lessons from *The 21 Laws of Influence* individually or group them together to become a master influencer. Practice, hone your skills, and use your common sense. Develop your own customized approach. Enjoy the influencing process and all of the benefits you will receive!

Good luck in your quest to increase your circle of influence!

CHAPTER 1

THE LAW OF AGENDAS

Those who control the program and set the deadlines are in the best position to influence the path taken to achieve their goals. Master influencers understand that those who control the agenda have more power over the process used to achieve the goal and most important, they have more control over the outcome.

Agendas outline a plan of action (the steps to be taken) to achieve goals. It is essential to share your agenda with others in order to establish unity and trust. Sharing helps to speed the influencing process. In meetings, your ability to control the agenda is usually directly proportional to the amount of influence you can exert.

Make it a priority to set the agenda (or at least contribute to it) whenever you need to influence the outcome. Be patient; move slowly, step by step. It may take time before you control the agenda, but it will be worth it! When you control the agenda, you can set the priorities and the time limits for reaching them. In many instances, when you control the agenda you can either influence or take charge of the accountability standards of the deliverables (agenda items). In addition, your opinions will carry greater weight and you take on authority when you take charge of the agenda.

 **Beware!**

Most managers quickly skim minutes and don't put sufficient time into evaluating them. Agendas and minutes are vital to the success of the company's goals. They keep employees and managers on track day after day, week after week. Stress to managers the importance of their fully understanding all agenda items because it's difficult to efficiently implement objectives that they many not completely understand. This is especially important when sabotage might rear its ugly head. Sometimes people just don't want to advance your agenda. An effective way of holding people accountable and monitoring their progress is through the agenda system. Prior to setting major goals and setting long-term strategies in motion, suggest off-premises "weekends" or retreats to provide a more relaxing atmosphere for your personnel to concentrate on setting priorities.

Also, beware that others do not take over the agenda for your project or goal. If they do obtain control of the agenda, they now hold the power. Now, your ability to influence the outcome is diminished. Masters of influence understand the importance of the agenda and will attempt to control it (and thereby control the goal process). Often they will attempt to insert their agenda items onto your agenda, perhaps even overpowering your influencing strategy, stalling your progress, and thwarting your goals. The lesson: Keep control of the agenda!

> To get to the Promised Land, you have to negotiate your way through the wilderness.
>
> **Herb Cohen, Negotiations Expert**

 THE PROBLEM

A corporation asked for my help with a cross-functional team that was achieving only 50% of its goals. The telecommunications team consisted of seven members. All of the team members were extremely bright and performed their individual job responsibilities exceptionally well, but every one of them was accustomed to operating independently. The goals for the team had been clearly defined and explained, but after six months, very few of the goals had been met. My task was to find out why so little had been accomplished and, if possible, to solve the problem.

STEPS

Step 1: Investigate

I interviewed several team members and examined how the team ran its meetings.

Step 2: Put someone in charge

I suggested assigning a team member to be in charge of putting together an agenda for the team's next meeting. I insisted on a clear process for compiling the agenda and required all input on the agenda be submitted to the person in charge at least 24 hours before each scheduled meeting. I warned team members that only the topics listed on the agenda would be discussed at the meeting and made it clear that any topics would be shelved -- no matter how great their importance -- until they were placed on the agenda through this <u>predetermined, structured, agreed-upon process</u>.

I explained that emergencies do come up and people will want (and need) to add to the agenda during the meeting and within the 24-hour rule. *Agendas should never lose their flexibility.* But, the team had to make a pact to stick with this process.

Before the item could be addressed, it must be put on the agenda. The team leader should be given the authority to determine whether the added item should be added or not according to team priorities and the plan. The goal was the individual to first ask before disrupting the agenda process: Could this wait until the next meeting or is it urgent? The team leader should question: Was it simply someone not adhering to the 24-hour rule (again!) or was it truly an exception that warranted time at this meeting?

Later in the process I taught the team to request 'people in attendance' so that we could structure and segment the agenda efficiently. The goal: If you didn't need to be there, you could leave the meeting and get other work done. People love this!

Step 3: Name a minutes keeper

I assigned a minutes keeper for the next meeting. The minutes keeper would take and compile minutes of the meeting and forward a copy of them to each team member within 24 hours of the meeting. The minutes would list all deliverables that were promised during the meeting, agenda items carried forward, and information about the upcoming meeting's agenda. Team members had one business day to respond to the minutes. Again, any input for the next meeting's agenda had to be submitted 24-hours prior to the meeting. The person also was required to ask for an appropriate amount of time for their agenda item with their agenda request.

Step 4: Rotate minutes keepers

A rotating schedule was established that gave each team member the opportunity to be the minute keeper/agenda compiler. I wanted them to realize how irritating it is when someone breaks the rules. To get the individuals to change their behavior, I needed the person to fully understand the process at the ground level. The team agreed to impose disciplinary action if the minutes keeper/agenda compiler does not fulfill the obligations in a timely manner. The team members also agreed, since they were a cross-functional team with limited authority to impose consequences on individual team members, that transgressions would be reported to the project manager immediately. It would be the project manager's responsibility to make note of the member's lapse on the individual's project performance report, which would be evaluated for their annual performance appraisal.

Step 5: Official record

I provided the team with a three-ring binder and informed them that the agenda would set out the official record of the team's goals and accountability metrics. At the start of each meeting, we would review every agenda item, promised deliverable, and time line. As I explained the process, half of the team members visibly relaxed. Why? Because they understood that we were wrapping processes and procedures around the team's goals.

When people have to work quickly and decisions are pressing, accountability takes on a larger role. It pinpoints roadblocks and identifies the responsible parties, which helps you make quicker, more cost-effective fixes. Accountability also helps reduce personnel turnover, which builds stability, and saves costly hiring expenses.

THE BOTTOM LINE

Two team members resisted both the agenda process and the minutes keeping process. After three meetings, I discovered why: These individuals were consistently failing to deliver on their promises to other team members during and after meetings. The agenda and minutes process was forcing them to be accountable for their promises. After some resistance and more than a little team communication, the reluctant members agreed to abide by the promises set forth in the agenda and the minutes. As soon as they came around, the team's productivity skyrocketed!

Expect some people to resist accountability.

14

After two years, the team membership had changed but the team remained highly productive. The team continues to use the agenda process to keep on track. In fact, the team became the poster children for how the corporation's teams should ideally operate.

As a result of the agenda process, communication became more effective and stress was significantly reduced. This occurred quickly because team members learned to trust one another and the agenda and minutes provided accountability for both individuals and the team.

Two team members were promoted to higher management levels. After the promotions, new members quickly assimilated into the team because the agendas and minutes gave them a record they could read to get up to speed and pick up where their predecessors left off.

INFLUENCE ILLUSTRATED

During the first six months of 1944, the United States, Great Britain and their allies assembled their land, air, and naval resources to prepare for 'Operation Overlord,' culminating in the invasion of Normandy. The goal was set – take full advantage of the strength of the allies' combined forces and begin the assault on Hitler's "Fortress Europe". The plans began to form in early 1943 for what would set the stage for the carefully choreographed D-Day invasion – the greatest joint task force ever assembled.

Long before the invasion took place on June 6th, 1944, the agenda included hundreds of line items. As the final days approached the agenda was updated, adjusted and refined. Some of the agenda items taken from historical documents from the Dwight D. Eisenhower Library are listed here:

- Photograph enemy defenses to gauge the strength of the German forces, bomb railroad lines along the French coastline, and drop supplies to the French Resistance to sustain the invading troops.
- Marshall over 5,000 vessels to assist with transporting troops for the assault and amass 12,000 planes to sweep the Luftwaffe from the skies.
- Create diversions to disperse German forces, sweep landing areas for mines and mark a path for amphibious vessels, and protect the flotilla as it crosses the English Channel.
- Coordinate all Allied Forces under a joint command and keep the location and the timing of the invasion secret.
- Establish communication and authority protocols and clearly communicate expectations, roles and responsibilities throughout the forces.
- Training -- nine army divisions (three airborne and six infantry) to perform – e.g. engineers to destroy beach obstacles, Rangers to scale cliffs, quartermasters to stockpile supplies, and infantrymen to wade through surf in treacherous conditions and conduct amphibious rehearsals.
- Ensure that the Soviets can tie down enemy troops on the Eastern Front and isolate battlefields for ground combat on the Northwestern Front.
- Attack Germany's industrial complex in concentrated barrages to destroy the German soldiers' and citizens' morale.

By setting a clear agenda, the allies were able to establish a strategic plan of action that when executed led to victory. Without an agenda, the invasion of Normandy would have been chaotic, not the highly coordinated, efficient attack that resulted. To succeed, you must plan your campaigns as if you were invading the beaches of Normandy, and that starts by setting the agenda.

CHAPTER 2

THE LAW OF ANALYSIS AND BENCHMARKING

People work harder and are more motivated toward accomplishing goals when they receive frequent feedback on their progress. Sporting events have scoreboards for a reason. People love to keep track of things that matter to them. On the flip side, if you want something to matter to someone, have them start keeping track of it. Why is it that cities become galvanized with sports teams when they start a losing or winning streak? Because the media makes the general population aware of the team's progress. Often, people who don't care about the team suddenly perk up when the scores are mentioned. Interesting how we've been programmed to track, analyze and benchmark progress when it is brought to our attention. The Law of Analysis and Benchmarking are at work – no matter how little we previously cared about the goal.

Employees have the right to know where they stand and to receive validation of their efforts. To progress, they need both approval and constructive criticism. To maximize their productivity, employees should be told where their contributions fit into the overall scheme of things and how their individual efforts directly affect the company's objectives. This is a basic principle in the Six Sigma process. When you discuss the value stream, the underlying philosophy is that the sum total of all the employees' individual efforts should significantly add to what the customer considers as 'value'.

Evaluation of the company's current state and its future state will set the direction for the company.

You can leverage the Law of Analysis and Benchmarking by simply understanding that employees are more willing to be influenced and to follow the leader's guidance when they are assured they are making good progress and their contributions are valued. Proof of progress boosts motivation. It also keeps people happy and on the right track.

As a manager, you have a fiduciary responsibility to deliver timely *ongoing* feedback *and* written *annual* performance evaluations for your direct reports. You are obligated to clearly state how well they have fulfilled their responsibilities according to your expectations. Therefore, it is incumbent upon you to clearly communicate up front to your people your goals, accountability metrics, and expectations.

Management must work to make employees smarter than they were yesterday and to help employees increase their income potential.

Beware!

Control your monitoring and evaluation costs. If you want to stay in business, the monitoring costs cannot exceed the return. Resist the urge to implement 'command and control' types of benchmarking and reporting processes. Be flexible with reporting processes for different levels of staff. Remember that goal-driven, highly motivated people might not need as much monitoring and evaluation as other employees. Too much evaluating, benchmarking, and reporting might cost you your best people.

Ask yourself:

- Is the correct process in place to improve productivity, track customer service, retain business, and expand our market presence without putting a burden on our employees or resources?

- Will the employee or manager benefit from tracking their progress?

- Will it help them grow? For example, by tracking a salesperson's referrals, can you see a pattern that is causing stress?

- Will the company benefit?

- Will the customers benefit?

- Use your common sense – if the answer is no, look at the benchmarking process. Does it make sense?

You can measure opportunity with the same yardstick that measures the risk involved.
They go together.

Earl Nightingale

INFLUENCE ILLUSTRATED

Three lobbyists were discussing how they would know that they had established influence with the White House.

Lobbyist 1 said that he would know that he had power if the President invited him to a private White House dinner.

Lobbyist 2 stated that he would consider himself influential if the President, during a private White House dinner, refused to interrupt their conversation in order to answer his personal hotline.

Lobbyist 3 declared that she would feel powerful if, during a private White House dinner, the hotline rang, the President answered it and said to her, "Here, it's for you".

 THE PROBLEM

To sustain a team's motivation to achieve its long-range goals.

STEPS

Step 1: Explain the goals

Clearly explain to team members the team's goals, the time lines, benchmarking periods, and clarify how their work fits into the specific project and company's overall objectives. As a manager, you must make sure those responsible understand the results you expect and the standards by which their efforts will be evaluated. Throughout the course of the project, reiterate the goals and your expectations.

Step 2: Provide feedback

Regularly provide feedback to team members on how both they and the team are progressing. Post charts that visually plot progress. To sustain motivation, employees need to see how they are doing. It helps keep people on track if you graphically depict where they are, where they came from and where they need to go. Take every opportunity to give deserved compliments, but don't give praise that was not earned or you will jeopardize your credibility. Give constructive criticism, feedback, and adequate direction in a manner that will encourage improvement, not disillusionment.

Step 3: Rate performance against expectations

To provide clear and consistent feedback, examine whether your people:

- **Exceed expectations**
  If your employees exceed expectations, congratulate them and ask if they would consider mentoring others. Also inquire if they have any suggestions regarding how their progress or other parts of the project could have been improved. Consider discussing with them how you can help them move further along in the company, if that is their goal.

- **Meet expectations**
  If employees simply met expectations, congratulate them and ask what problems they incurred and how they think their performance could be improved. If you think they might be capable of exceeding expectations, pay careful attention to whether they fully understand the project goals and/or whether they might need further training or assistance. After the goal is accomplished, if they didn't exceed expectations this time, perhaps next time they will exceed the requirements if you do this.

- **Need improvement**
  First find out if your explanation of the goals and objectives was clear and whether the employee fully understood what you wanted. You are responsible for making your employees understand. Always remember: People will often indicate that they understand *when they do not* in order to avoid appearing foolish or stupid. Check their comprehension of your expectations; especially if you are addressing a new employee or team member. Do this with sensitivity! Never appear patronizing or look like you do not trust the person's listening skills.

  If you find that the person did not understand you, ask yourself, "What can I do in the future to make sure they understand me?" Be a smart leader -- transfer some of the responsibility for the communication to the other person. Stress to the employee that it is crucial that they clearly understand your expectations. Tell them that it is *their responsibility to question you* about anything that they don't fully understand. If they do this in the future, make sure you show that this is okay and expected!

Specifically ask if they feel that your expectations cannot be met and find out the reasons for their answers. Perhaps you set the bar too high or gave them insufficient time, help or training. Create an open and cordial atmosphere where they feel comfortable approaching you. Emphasize that their performance rating may depend on the clarity of the communications between you. The employee must take responsibility for understanding your expectations and requirements. If they have questions or areas they think need clarification, they must ask!

Finally, be brutally honest. Ask yourself: Do I have the right person in the right position?

 # THE BOTTOM LINE

In order to grow professionally, people need consistent feedback to measure their progress regarding the expectations they are hired to fulfill. They need yardsticks to see where they stand. Make feedback a standard part of your management techniques or your workplace might resemble a revolving door.

CHAPTER 3

THE LAW OF BELIEF REPLACEMENT

People are willing to change their beliefs ONLY when they are replaced by other beliefs that, at the very least, are equally as valid in their minds. To change people's minds, make a suggestion and then introduce a solution.

Most people will not change unless you can provide them with an alternative that is equally or more convincing than those they presently hold. A new belief, concept, or approach is more likely to be accepted when you can convincingly demonstrate the added benefits that the new position will bring.

 **Beware!**

If upper management does not truly accept the new methods or beliefs, sooner or later the employees will revert to the old ways. Initially, they may give lip service to the new, especially if they think it's politically expedient, and they might even go through the motions. However, when the opportunity is ripe, they will go back to the old, which will probably undermine your efforts to create change.

The greatest discovery of my generation is that human beings can alter their lives by altering their attitudes of mind.

William James

 THE PROBLEM

The Executive Vice President (EVP) of one of the world's largest defense contractor wanted to change the culture of his division from a command and control driven system to a cooperative, matrix-based approach. However, most division managers balked because they did not believe that releasing control over employees would make the organization more productive. They believed that they had to tell their employees exactly what to do, precisely when to do it, and insisted on having the final say on how jobs were done. Their approach created numerous bottlenecks; it frustrated the workforce, morale suffered, and attrition rose. The organization bogged down. Some of the best employees left and many joined competitors.

STEPS

Step 1: Gather background information

I met with the EVP who said he was tired of telling his managers how NOT to think. He expected the managers to pick up the ball and make those fundamental changes necessary to move the organization forward.

Step 2: Explore alternatives

I asked the EVP, "Have you told them what they should be thinking?" I explained that I found it beneficial to suggest to employees <u>what they should be thinking</u> AFTER I explain <u>what I no longer want them to think</u>. With that, the EVP replied, "I've just been telling them what not to do. Maybe I should start telling them what I want them to do and what I need them to believe."

Step 3: Importance and consequences

I also suggested, "Tell them why it's so important that they believe in your new vision for the new way of doing business. Sometimes, it's best to spell out the consequences of their current behavior and actions and how they impact your goals. You have to do this so that they can understand your vision and your expectations of them. Set out the two paths that you currently see."

- "First, explain the corporate ramifications and personal consequences if they continue doing business as normal and of continuing in their old management ways. Second, emphasize that the organization must change for the well being of the employees and for the corporation's long-term viability. Also, point out why their adherence to their current beliefs will be detrimental to themselves, their employees, and the organization. Bottom line: Make sure they embrace your leadership philosophy and get with the program!"

- "For the managers," I continued, "Their performance evaluations should suffer because they were unsuccessful in retaining key employees, especially those who went with competitors. Let them know they will be held accountable for both attracting AND retaining key personnel. Furthermore, low morale often equates to low employee productivity and you might remind them that their security as a manager is tied to their department's performance."

- Finally, I recommended that he discuss with managers the consequences of not changing with the organization. Losing top people to a competitor hurts business. These people have specialized knowledge that customers depend on for delivering their products. When customers learn that key employees are unhappy working with the company, they might just question why they're still doing business with you – especially when the employees are moving over to your competitor. Perhaps the employees know something that they -- as the customers -- don't and should!"

Step 4: Spread the word

The EVP and I then put together a road show for his management team. At the same time, we distributed a heartbeat survey to the organization to establish a baseline for change. We agreed to travel across the country to managers' locations to deliver clear, concise messages on the consequences of sticking with their current management style. We explained the consequences of not changing and refusing to move forward with their leader's vision for the future.

We gave the managers (1) succinct, comprehensible goals and objectives with (2) firm deadlines for their results. We combined this timetable with (3) a training program designed to teach the managers how to move from a command and control management style to a more cooperative, fluid, and agile management style.

The EVP clearly stressed his objectives and stated in no uncertain terms why it was so crucial for his management team to change. He explained that only by changing their current mindsets and moving forward could they improve their management techniques.

Step 5: Begin training

Six weeks after the road show, the management team entered a training program that cemented the new, more desirable beliefs into their psyches.

Step 6: Evaluate progress

Three months after running the management seminars, we assessed the management team's progress by conducting another heartbeat survey and reviewing whether the attrition numbers changed.

Fortunately, attrition slowed significantly and we were satisfied that the Belief Replacement strategy was working.

Were we able to change most managers' mindsets? Yes, although a few chose not to come around. Overall, we were able to convert most managers because we explained, and they understood, the consequences of not changing and how it would impact the company, their employees, and themselves.

INFLUENCE ILLUSTRATED

Most of Victor Seribriakoff's teachers predicted that he would never finish school and branded him a "dunce". So he lived up to their expectations by dropping out of school and spending the next 17 years trying to find his place in life. At age 32, Victor learned that he had a 161 I.Q.; he was a genius! Although he was initially astounded, Victor accepted the fact and began living like a genius. He started writing, inventing, and engaging in many successful business ventures. His greatest accomplishment, the pinnacle of his altered belief in himself, came when he was elected chairman of the international Mensa Society, a group that requires members to have an I.Q. of at least 140.

CHAPTER 4

THE LAW OF COMMITMENT

People are more likely to listen to you (and subsequently trust you) if they see you take action directed at achieving your goals. If you prove your dedication to your goals, others will understand that you are committed and that you are true to your word. Actions speak louder than words.

Employees tend to follow those who have clear and specific goals. They want to be inspired; to feel the power and passion of your commitment. Instead of just saying "I'm going to run a marathon someday", be specific and say, "I'm going to run the Boston Marathon next year in ___ time." When you precisely identify your goals, it holds weight; when you write it down, it holds greater weight. If you state your goal, write it down, and then act on it, chances are that more people will be influenced; and you will accomplish your goal.

Commitment demonstrates your personal involvement. It shows how highly you value what you seek. It exhibits how far you will go to achieve your objectives. Your commitment is your most effective tool in influencing others to support you, your program, service, or goal. Commitment conveys the feeling of permanence and it increases the likelihood that you will achieve your goals.

Visit the floor where the product is made to say "hello". Stop by and speak with personnel in all departments.

Show involvement in every segment of the business, even if it's something that you don't know or understand --- it can improve your education. It also demonstrates your willingness to learn from your employees – great leaders understand the value of the information you glean from 'management by walking around'.

 Beware!

Some individuals who commit subsequently become reluctant to change, even in light of overwhelming evidence. Remember, all things change and wise business operators adjust accordingly. Great leaders recognize that the most prudent course of action may be to cut their losses, even when their investment is great. Over-committing can cloud a leader's judgment regarding when to surrender, pull back, cut losses, or terminate underperforming employees. It can restrict a manager's ability to be impartial and objective. It also fosters rigid thinking and can stifle innovation.

When things don't 'feel' right or the numbers are going south, ask yourself: "Is our commitment to this project clouding our judgment?" Often, the key to attaining goals is making smaller commitments instead of locking onto unwavering commitments. Committing to small incremental goals provides flexibility to make needed changes. This isn't to say that you are undecided about achieving the end goal; this way of thinking simply gives you flexibility and allows you to keep your mind open to change. Having a plan to benchmark while committing is the key to balancing the effects of the Law of Commitment.

> The first rule of success, and the one that supersedes all others, is to have energy. It is important to know how to concentrate it, how to husband it, how to focus it on important things instead of frittering it away on trivia.
>
> **MICHAEL KORDA**

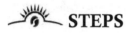 ## THE PROBLEM

In the face of cutthroat competition, a large national chain wanted to distinguish itself from the pack and increase its retail store sales by building customers' loyalty.

STEPS

Step 1: Formulate a Strategy

The management team firmly committed to a policy to increase customer satisfaction. By providing superior customer service, the company influenced customers to conduct repeat business with its stores. The management team understood that initially customers often purchase small items and if their experience is good, customers are more likely to return to purchase costlier items. Customer satisfaction is especially critical with businesses that sell high-ticket items.

Step 2: Make it a habit

Management drilled its customer satisfaction policy into the heads of all new employees until it became second nature to them. Management constantly monitors each employee's performance. It is benchmarked against the strict customer service parameters that have been established in the training sessions. As a rule, the company's personnel smile at customers, are friendly and polite, and all employees are expected to be exceptionally helpful. Expect the results to happen if you deliver according to your strategy.

Step 3: Anticipate the worst

In your commitment to customer satisfaction, always be prepared for the worst. Have policies in place for dealing with the unexpected because disasters always occur. When they do, don't blame others.

Contact your client or customer and:
A. Admit the problem occurred.
B. Apologize, express your sorrow, and state what caused the problem, if you know.
C. If you don't know why the problem occurred, state that you've begun an investigation in to the cause in order to assure that it won't happen again.
D. Clearly and calmly explain the steps you have taken to fix the problem and to put safeguards in place that will guarantee that it won't happen again. AND
E. Take full responsibility for the problem and reiterate that you will do whatever it takes to prevent its reoccurrence.

THE BOTTOM LINE

The chain has remained extremely successful even in tough times. Repeat business is at the core of the company's success. Its commitment to customer satisfaction fosters customer loyalty, which equates to future sales revenue. I have been doing business with the company for more than 15 years and although I have had a few defective products, I have never had a problem returning products or getting a product fixed.

INFLUENCE ILLUSTRATED

To build its customer base, Southwest Airline's management team made a commitment to institute a humor policy aimed at ensuring that its passengers had fun and enjoyed traveling on Southwest flights. Flight attendants joked with customers, donned crazy hats, and wore Halloween costumes. Cabin crewmembers might announce, "Let's get boarded now, sure and steady wins the race, but quick as you can makes us fly faster! It's cold as sin here but where we're headed it's 30 degrees warmer. So, sinners to the back, all others grab a seat in the front pews! Let's get this bird in the air!"

However, after the tragic events of 9/11, Southwest changed its policy because the use of humor seemed inappropriate. Then, nearly a year and a half later, management decided that their passengers and staff would accept a return to its old jovial, unconventional behavior. In reversing its policy, the management team told personnel to be extremely sensitive to passengers. Employees were instructed to err on the side of caution and avoid humor if, for any reason, they or passengers felt uncomfortable.

At Southwest, the commitment to humor runs deep. At job interviews, candidates are assessed regarding their views on humor. They may be asked, "Have you ever used humor in the workplace? Have you diffused a potentially negative workplace situation by using humor? Have you seen others use humor to help someone through a particularly sensitive event?"

CHAPTER 5

The Law of Consistency

People are more willing to trust those who behave in a stable and predictable manner. A person who exhibits a high degree of consistency is often perceived as trustworthy, powerful, and intelligent. Consistency has the effect of lowering a person's defenses in favor of your ability to influence them. Organizations should replicate this same philosophy to influence people to gain employee and customer trust.

We tend to trust people who are consistent. Because their behavior and words are consistent and predictable, we allow them to influence us without much resistance. Consistent people do not constantly change their behavior, communication style, goals, or manner of doing business. They don't waver or waffle, and they appear stable. We know where they stand. Once we understand their values and how they operate, we can rely upon them to do as we expect.

In most societies, trust and consistency are synonymous. A high level of consistency is considered honorable, while inconsistency is linked with distrust, dishonesty, indecisiveness, and negative behavior. Employees will avoid contact with inconsistent managers, which, in turn, may create distrust, impair communications, increase the likelihood of mistakes, trigger misunderstandings, and dampen morale.

Consistency relates to actions more than to words. Many people will say anything to achieve their goals. These people don't mean what they say – they know they are being devious but they simply don't care. Haven't we all encountered characters who didn't deliver *what* they promised and/or *when* they promised? Their behavior, not their words, showed us who they are. The other person's behavior was our primary source of information about their beliefs, values, and attitudes.

Because there are so many people who have duped us along the way, when we finally perceive that someone has a high degree of consistency, we tend to let this aspect of their personality potentially cloud our judgment; or perhaps let it lower our defenses when we normally wouldn't in a similar situation with another person. We let the 'consistent' person influence us without thinking that what we are currently seeing might not be consistent with our favorable past experience with the individual. In other words, we let the Law of Consistency take over when we should be vigilant, or at least cautious.

Another aspect of the Law of Consistency is that the more we comply with the person, the more chance they have to make us willing to comply again. The pattern is slowly but surely established as the Law of Consistency sucks us in.

These last examples illustrate the negative side of the Law of Consistency. Basically the Law of Consistency states that people will feel compelled to be influenced in a similar way if they have complied with a similar request in the past.

Non-profit organizations have long known the power of the Law of Consistency. They know that the best person to get charitable donations from is a person who has given to their charity (or a similar organization) previously. Telemarketers are trained to ask "for just a moment of your time to complete a survey" then they ask for "just another minute to ask another question". Before long, you've been on the line five minutes and they are pitching their product, service, political organization, or scheme.

How do you make sure the Law of Consistency is not being used against you? Ask yourself: "Would I do this if this were a stand-alone request? Will complying with this request make me want to kick myself later? Am I just doing this because they expect me to because I've done this for them previously?"

Peer pressure can also play a major role in influencing consistency. Behavior can be affected by the overwhelming urge to be consistent with peers --- the societal pressure to look, act, and feel as they do. Unfortunately, the peer pressure of wanting to be accepted can also cause some people to act in ways that may conflict with their values and morals.

A powerful way to leverage the Law of Consistency is to realize that if you want people to go along with your goals or agree to a request, simply ask them first to agree to a smaller request before asking them to comply with the more important solicitation. Get them comfortable with saying "yes". Simply stated: Start with a smaller request, get a 'yes', and then build up to a bigger 'yes'. You may find that it is most effective to build multiple smaller 'yes' requests into your influencing strategy if your goal is to ask the person for a large request. For example: When the goal is to lock down a multi-year large charitable donation, first invite the other person to become a board member, then ask for the donation. If you need commitment for a substantial life insurance policy, ask for a financial planning fee for preparing the documents. If you want management to support a substantially different philosophy, get buy in for the plan by showing smaller results in targeted areas before you implement the philosophy throughout the corporation. If you are requesting that your boss commit substantial resources to your project, stage a series of 'yes' requests throughout your presentation instead of asking for the whole ball of wax at once. If you are a team leader who needs people to give up vacation time to finish a program, ask team members for a couple of nights first so that they can understand the importance of getting the project out the door -- no matter what. Once they have agreed to Wednesday, follow up with the next appeal.

Because of habit patterns associated with the Law of Consistency, people will tend to say 'yes' more often if you use this approach.

 Beware!

Consistency makes people comfortable and often resistant to change. They are hesitant to go out on a limb to learn something new. Why should they when the old ways get the job done? They really don't care that the change will make it better. They like the status quo. People also tend to feel threatened when they are asked to change.

To facilitate change:
- Move incrementally -- sometimes you have to say "yes" when you want to say "no". Ask yourself, "Is the Law of Consistency holding me back?" Make the Law of Consistency work in your favor. Make (and communicate) smaller, consistent changes that lead to the eventual goal rather than overwhelming people with too much, too soon. Too much information given when people aren't ready to listen often causes undue resistance and only makes your job that much more difficult.
- Build upon existing processes and institutions so that the process is not too jarring and abrupt.
- Frame requests for change in terms of your employee's education, growth and advancement.
- Stress the benefits of changing and the consequences of staying put.

Remember that many corporate employees have been subjected to all sorts of changes. As a result, they may interpret your requests as the "flavor of the month", and stick to their old ways because they expect management to come up with another 'new initiative' next week, or look at your goal as 'change du jour".

INFLUENCE ILLUSTRATED

In January 1943, at Casablanca, the decision to invade Sicily all but ensured that the Mediterranean would continue to be the main theater in Europe during 1943. During this period, British influence and the logic of continuing with the momentum in the area guaranteed that the focus swung away from conflict in northwestern Europe. However, what most people do not know is that these events delayed "Operation Overlord," the invasion of Normandy.

At the time, the American high command was alarmed by the British generals' persistent pressure to broaden the Mediterranean front and extend eastward when they had promised to focus on the cross-Channel invasion. American military leaders began to lose trust in the British when they refused to give "overriding priority" to the invasion plan as they had consistently promised to do in the past. This further cemented the Americans' misgivings. The Americans became less communicative and less trusting with every inconsistency. They began formulating their own plans without consulting the Brits. The deteriorating trust issue between the two began to affect others and the Soviets threatened to pull out and topple Germany without the Allies.

At the Cairo meetings, the stage was set for a showdown. "It is certainly an odd way of helping the Russians," Churchill declared in a barbed comment to the Americans insistence on the sanctity of the plans for "Operation Overlord." The British leadership told the Americans, "We must not... regard Overlord on a fixed date as the pivot of our whole strategy on which all else turns." The Americans thought otherwise and it took two months to put the invasion plans back on track. The date we remember – June 6th, 1944 – should have been months earlier. It was postponed because of the effects of the Law of Consistency.

You will have a harder time influencing others if you are inconsistent with your actions and goals. Be consistent and prove that others should follow your lead!

If you have an important point to make, don't try to be subtle or clever. Use a pile driver. Hit the point once. Then come back and hit it again. Then, a third time, a tremendous whack.

Winston Churchill

 THE PROBLEM

To encourage personnel to perform their tasks in a consistent manner, while allowing them to retain sufficient flexibility to make needed changes.

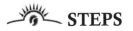 STEPS

Step 1: Communication counts

Clearly communicate and periodically reiterate the goals until the desired results are achieved. Use the same words, tonality, and gestures to reiterate your message. Try to highlight the same points again and again whenever you discuss the progress of the project and the goal. Keep doing this throughout the process so that your audiences know that your message is consistent.

Step 2: Behave in a consistent manner

When your team understands how you act in various situations, they will know the standards you demand. On the basis of your responses to their past behavior, they will realize how you expect them to act. Most important, when you're not around, your employees will replicate how you would act with customers, peers, upper-level management, and co-workers. Your consistent behavior will spawn their consistent behavior.

Over time, the consistent standards you demand will be woven into the fabric of your organization's culture. They become the cultural norms that will form the basis for your employees' behavior. Employees will respond automatically to recurrent situations, which will make them more efficient. Their responses will also program new employees to meet those standards you have consistently set.

Consistency and automatic responses do not overly tax employees, especially in the performance of menial or mundane tasks. This can free their minds to concentrate on more important issues such as problem solving, innovation, and strategies that can enhance profits and customer services.

Step 3: Acknowledge or reward

Commend employees or give them monetary rewards for coming up with productive changes. For example, when they make suggestions for process improvements, cost cutting, or streamlining paperwork, practices, and procedures.

Step 4: Document successes

Maintain records showing how consistency has been beneficial to personnel and the company. When possible translate the successes into the dollar amounts that were made or saved as a result of consistent actions and procedures.

Step 5: Remain flexible and open to change

Consistency can cause employees to become so entrenched in their ways that change might require Herculean efforts. Employees might resist change and complain, "That's the way we've always done it." They could feel threatened because consistency creates security.

Step 6: Consistently explain your inconsistencies

When you deviate from what you have previously told others you would do, or you exhibit behavior that might be perceived as contrary to your goals, explain the reasons for the change to your employees. This will teach them about how you make decisions. They are gaining knowledge of how your reasoning mechanisms operate. When you explain changes in direction, your staff will learn when taking different routes would be justified (and appropriate if you were in their shoes).

Step 7: Continually monitor consistency patterns

Use simple performance ratings, not complex numerical systems that cannot be understood. You want understanding, so keep it simple.

 ## THE BOTTOM LINE

If not monitored, consistency can cause complacency, laziness, and inefficiency. To be certain that the Law of Consistency is working effectively, always:

- Identify all consistent behavior patterns.

- Question the validity of all consistent behavior patterns and examine whether other approaches might be more effective. If so, implement the preferred approaches with the team.

- Provide consistent role models as examples of desired team and employee behavior.

- Build trust through consistent actions.

- Make certain that employees understand the overall goals and objectives of the department and of the corporation.

CHAPTER 6

The Law of Contrast

When the contrast between alternatives is great, it is easier to convince people to take one path rather than the other. The differences between two opposed ideas are more apparent when the ideas are presented at the same time and the contrasts are emphasized.

Often, the differences between ideas or approaches seem insignificant. However, when they are presented at the same time, the differences between them can appear to be at opposite ends of the spectrum. To make one alternative more appealing, increase the degree of separation, compare the ends of the spectrum and point out how they differ.

Ben Franklin was a master of influence. One of his favorite tools was the Law of Contrast. He eloquently and diplomatically pointed out the pros and cons of different ideas in order to lead people in his direction. Time and again, he used contrasting points to make his point, swaying the minds of those who opposed him and his ideals. Franklin's ability to influence in this manner was precisely why the Continental Congress selected him to be the Ambassador to France when the fledgling United States needed a strong European ally in its bid for independence.

 **Beware!**

The Law of Contrasts can be used against you so recognize when people make your goals look insignificant by contrasting your objectives to their loftier aspirations. This occurs frequently when departments vie for budget money.

Insurance salespeople are taught to reduce premiums to ridiculous amounts. For example, if a policy costs $750 a year, the salesperson might equate the outlay to less than "$2.00 a day – not even the price of a child's happy meal!"

When you recognize that the Law of Contrast is in play, reverse the tactic by simply reversing the process and spinning it back with a contrast that supports your goals. Make the salesperson prove that their product is the correct choice for your needs. To open up dialog with an insurance salesperson and stop them from using the Law of Contrast to influence you during the sales process, do your research and come prepared with pertinent questions. You might ask, "Yes, but what would a decreasing term insurance policy cost? If we could buy a different policy and invest what we save, might that be a better strategy? Even if we save $1.00 a day ($30/month) it amounts to $365 a year – that's a lot of money over thirty years! If we could get an 8% return it would be nearly $45,000. Not bad for $1.00 a day!"

There are two kinds of people, those who do the work and those who take the credit. Try to be in the first group, there is less competition there.

Indira Gandhi.

INFLUENCE ILLUSTRATED

A group of vagrants had the brilliant idea to sell a magic life sustaining elixir to the local townspeople. Although they could not create a potion that actually extended life, they poured water into colored bottles and claimed it was specially formulated to increase longevity while still maintaining the clean and refreshing taste of water.

As soon as the elixir went on sale, the townspeople rushed to purchase it. They were astounded that the price was $10.00 a bottle, which was equivalent to a week of hard labor. "By paying ten dollars today, you'll live at least 50 years longer! This is just twenty cents a year up front and you can live to see your great grandchildren come into adulthood," they were advised.

So, the excited townspeople bought the entire supply of magic elixir. When all the bottles were sold, the vagrants decided to take their earnings and get out of town. When the townspeople saw no changes from their use of the elixir, the vagrants who took their money were long gone. They were now selling magic potion in a neighboring town for just "$12.00 a bottle for a longer life!"

☀ THE PROBLEM

A profitable, high-tech manufacturing facility was ordered to cut its headcount across-the-board by 12%. The facility's managers felt that the cut was ill advised in light of the fact that for the last two years, the facility returned 60% higher profits than anticipated. Plus, it was only one of three manufacturing facilities that produced the company's most profitable products. I was brought in to help the managers craft a message to the employees.

Management at the facility was baffled at why the cut was requested at their plant because their people were routinely working overtime every week. The site was profitable and orders were flowing in. They had more work than they could handle with the staff they had now. How could somebody be asking them to cut people? They pleaded with the corporate Vice President of Human Relations but all it produced was frustration. The question was: How could we stop morale from tanking and inform already overworked workers that they were going to be expected to perform even more work?

☀ STEPS

Step 1: Reconsider the approach

I suggested that before making an announcement to the employees, management should take another stab at changing the rules for the reduction in force (RIF).

Step 2: Listen to the words

I instructed the Facility Vice President to listen carefully when he discussed the impending RIF with the VP of HR. Specifically, I requested that he write down the exact words the Corporate VP used and the reasons he stated.

The Facility VP noticed that the Corporate VP repeatedly said, "only a 12% reduction" whenever he spoke of the headcount issue. When the Facility VP referred to the reduction as the loss of more than 80 workers, the VP of Human Resources didn't budge. He countered by pointing out that another facility had been forced to cut 93 people. He continually repeated the term "only 12%," thereby invoking the Law of Contrast to make 12% seem like a small fraction when compared to a worst-case scenario of a 100% plant closure. Twice he mentioned that it was management's responsibility to keep the lights on throughout the whole corporation and to make a profit. He also stated, "The only way to be fair about cutting costs and to achieve the headcount goal was to do an across-the-board cut at all the plants".

Step 3: Reword the facts

Our strategy was to use the Law of Contrast to our benefit – since the VP of HR was using it for his, we had to make the impact of the reduction look big! But, how? I counseled the management team to convert the headcount percentages into man-hours. Every hour the employees worked could be measured in direct profit to the whole corporation. So, I recommended that the management team put together a new presentation for the Corporate VP of HR.

With a potential loss of 80 people for this layoff, working an average of 50 hours per week (40 regular plus 10 hours of overtime), it was easy to do the calculations. For 80 employees who worked 50 weeks a year -- the total came to a potential annual loss of **200,000 profitable man-hours**. Once we had calculated this incredible number, we translated it into language we knew would make sense to the corporate VP. The team calculated those 200,000 man-hours in terms of the profits they could prove that each employee generated per hour. The profits created per employee were $15.57 per hour, which when multiplied by 200,000 man-hours equaled a total of $3,114,000 per year.

When the financial manager delivered the numbers, even the management team was shocked at the scope of the potential loss they were facing! Then, they figured out that without that profit, their bonuses were on the line, too! Convincing corporate to reverse their thinking started to become a fight for their financial survival.

Step 4: Put forth your argument

The Facility VP then arranged a conference call with the Corporate VP. Each time the Corporate VP said "only 12%," the Facility VP quickly injected the true impact number, $3,114,000. At every opportunity he reiterated, "It's not 12%. Sam, this is a direct loss of $3,114,000 in profits!" Suddenly the message got through. The VP of HR said, "I didn't realize that we'd potentially lose that much money by doing this to your plant. The goal is to save money and be more efficient, not to decrease profits!"

"Sam, I know that you think the only fair way to get your headcount number is to do an across-the-board cut at all the facilities. I can see the logic in that way of thinking, but I think we should run the numbers on the impact on our bottom line and profits -- not just headcount. Listen, I'm only asking you to look at this another way with an open mind before we pull the trigger at my facility."

THE BOTTOM LINE

The Corporate VP soon agreed that enacting a twelve percent across-the-board workforce reduction was not worth losing over $3 million in profits from one location and demoralizing a profit-making workforce. In exchange for no cuts in personnel, the manufacturing facility's management team agreed to freeze hiring and to reduce headcount proportionally if profit margins dipped during the next 12 months.

NOTE: As a result of this event, the corporation reaped a more profound benefit. All facilities now understand that they are independently accountable for their numbers. Before, accountability for profits was pooled across the sites into one 'bucket'. Now, accountability for profits and staffing is placed correctly, with the individual sites.

CHAPTER 7

THE LAW OF EXPECTATION

People are pleased when they get more than they anticipated. They are disappointed when they do not receive what they expect. Go above and beyond what is expected to gain the influencing advantage.

Be realistic. Set your expectations not on the basis of your hopes and desires but on the abilities and limitations of those who are expected to perform. When both parties share and agree upon their objectives, the ability to influence will be enhanced.

Expectation and disappointment go hand-in-hand – when expectations are not met, trust and faith are lost – and as a result the power to influence decreases. So, temper your expectations of others and raise your expectations of yourself.

Most important, if you use the Law of Expectation to your advantage, you will recognize the power of the phrase, "Always under promise and over deliver." However, if you consistently over deliver on promises, the Law of Consistency will kick in and your reputation for being a 'great over deliverer' might hurt you. Why? Because you raised the bar! Don't be surprised if your customers, peers, teammates, or boss start to expect you to always over deliver and get upset if you 'only deliver' what you promised.

To avoid unrealistic expectations, try not to over deliver all the time. However, when you do, over deliver in varying amounts. Give 5%, then 12%, then 3%; don't become predictable. When appropriate, explain the reasons for the over delivery and state exactly how much extra effort was involved in delivering the job on Monday rather than on Tuesday. Point out how much it cost you in overtime, what special circumstances were involved and that your staff worked until 2:00 AM to make sure the report went out on time. Let it slip that you incurred additional expenses to keep them happy, but be subtle.

When you sense that your clients or customers always expect you to over deliver, remind them of the agreed upon terms and recalibrate their thinking. Set them straight. Do it sooner rather than later – before what you promised becomes less than they expect. Be clear about your obligations and correct any unrealistic expectations they may state. Clarity is the key to building great relationships.

 Beware!

Expectations cannot always be met – so be prepared and have a back-up plan. When you have good reason to believe that your hopes may not be fulfilled, accept it. Don't throw in the towel, but start directing your time, energy and resources on other options that could bring you closer to your goals.

> We love to expect, and when expectation is either disappointed or gratified, we want to be again expecting.
>
> **Samuel Johnson**

INFLUENCE ILLUSTRATED

Thomas Edison was approached by Western Union to buy his newly invented telegraph. Not certain of how much to charge for it, Edison asked for and received a few days to think about the purchase price. Edison discussed the offer with his wife, and although astounded by her suggestion to ask $20,000 for his invention, he agreed to do so.

Upon meeting with the Western Union representative Edison was dumbstruck. When asked for his price, he could not vocalize that he wanted $20,000 for his invention. Instead, he sat in silence. Exasperated, the Western Union official floated an offer of $100,000.

Edison took the offer.

THE PROBLEM

An internal position reopened that a good friend of mine had applied for a year before. Although she did not get the job last year, she had been on the short-list. The job required one credential that she had subsequently acquired and therefore she was invited to apply again. In the interim, she took a position working with a new supervisor. At that moment, she was especially pleased with her present situation. Her supervisor was attentive, respectful, honest, and direct. They were close, shared a positive working relationship, and enjoyed a good rapport outside the office.

Before deciding whether to apply, she wanted to get her supervisor's feedback and his thoughts on how it would affect her happiness, stress, effectiveness, and career advancement. Her supervisor knew that she had previously sought the job and was also aware that management was seriously considering her for the open position. My friend expected her supervisor to **know** that she **needed** his advice and direction, but when he didn't volunteer to help she became disappointed and angry. For several days she never asked for his advice, but she expected him to sense (read her mind!) that she would appreciate his guidance and input. Day after day, when he did not address the issue, she left work feeling neglected and confused. To compound matters, she questioned the strength of her relationship with her supervisor.

I counseled her to speak about her expectations and disappointment directly with her boss. We went over the steps I suggested she take.

 **STEPS**

Step 1: Schedule a conference

The next day, my friend asked to speak with her supervisor privately.

Step 2: State your expectations

When they met, she expressed her desire to get his opinion on the job and her consideration of the position. She explained how important his opinion was in her decision. She told him that she valued his council and that she was afraid to leave something that she liked to jump into something new.

Step 3: Keep an open mind and listen to the other side

He was open and honest with her. He explained that the reason he felt he could not offer her advice was that he was biased. He had a conflict of interest. On a business level, he told her that if she left he knew his boss would hold him accountable for the impact her leaving would cause the department. As a friend, he wanted her to go for the promotion, but knew that it would be difficult for her because the department she was going to lead was in a sorry state. It would be draining on her emotionally and extremely time consuming. Also, her promotion also meant a transfer to another city. She would be lonely and he knew her family would miss her. Yet, he wanted her to succeed and the company needed her.

Step 4: Strive for understanding

As he spoke, she started to understand his dilemma. The conversation was good for both of them.

Step 5: Attain closure and talk about lessons learned

My friend laughed and explained that she had stressed herself out unnecessarily. She told him that she wished she had been more open with him about her expectations. She promised to communicate better next time. Her boss said he would try to see the situation from her perspective and to improve his communication. Her boss gave her wonderful feedback and insights about the new job and gave her the confidence she needed to strive ahead. She left his office with a feeling of calm and a sense of direction.

 **THE BOTTOM LINE**

My friend realized that she expected her supervisor to know that she wanted his feedback and guidance. However, after meeting with him, she understood that it was unrealistic to expect him to read her mind because she had never communicated her feelings to him. Her unrealistic expectations created a barrier in their initial communications. A vital piece of information was missing -- her expectations. Their channels of communication were blocked until she told him what she expected.

CHAPTER 8

THE LAW OF EXPERTISE

People are more likely to listen to, trust, believe, and follow those who are acknowledged experts in their fields. Individuals who have demonstrated their expertise tend to exert more influence and command greater remuneration. When given the choice, people prefer to deal with experts and will pay for the privilege.

Most people defer to those they consider experts -- even to the point of not questioning the expert's logic or mental processes. They defer simply because the person is perceived as an expert, because of their reputation. Once people consider you an expert in your field, they will also tend to solicit your advice (because they perceive you as an authority) in arenas that may be out of your realm of expertise.

People like to deal with experts because it gives them greater assurance that the job will be done correctly, which in the long run can save them time, money, and aggravation. They gladly pay steep premiums to hire experts and love to declare, "I hired the best _____." Some might even take delight in broadcasting how much that expert charged. Dealing with experts elevates their status; it implies that they must be smart, financially secure, well connected, or special to be involved with the best.

 **Beware!**

Are you allowing yourself to be influenced by someone who is not really an authority on the subject? For example, entertainers often use their fame to pontificate about politics. These people use their skills as entertainers to assist in giving us the perception that they speak with authority when discussing foreign affairs, political matters, and the nation's agenda. However, if you took their expertise on political matters into consideration, you would usually find that the majority of entertainers are hardly experts. The depth of political reasoning we expect from an expert is lacking. The actor's skill in speaking in an authoritative manner and our own perception of them as experts in the entertainment business clouds our judgment. It leaves us open targets for influence! This doesn't mean I am saying that entertainers can't voice their opinion. I am just suggesting that it is wise to look at their knowledge of the subject matter before we grant them the right to influence us.

It is wise to adopt this philosophy whenever we listen to others voice opinions. We should always ask: "What is their knowledge of the subject? Are they an expert? Should I allow their opinion to sway me because they possess specialized knowledge of the issue? Am I transferring their status as an expert in one area over to this issue without the transfer of the status being warranted?" If you consistently ask yourself these types of questions, you will ensure that you are influenced more by facts than the opinions from people who are not authorities.

> It is the province of knowledge to speak, and it is the privilege of wisdom to listen.
>
> **Oliver Wendell Holmes, Jr.**

INFLUENCE ILLUSTRATED

Charlie Steinmetz had an "electronic mind". He designed and built the electrical generators in Henry Ford's first plant in Dearborn, Michigan and was an acknowledged mechanical expert.

When the generators at the Dearborn plant stopped running properly, Ford called in a number of mechanics and electricians, but they had no idea how to fix the problem. In desperation, he called Steinmetz, who tinkered around for a few hours and restored power.

Ford was delighted that the plant was up and running again, but he was astounded by Steinmetz's $10,000 bill. He sent the bill back to Steinmetz with a note that said, "Charlie, isn't this a little steep for a few hours of tinkering?"

Steinmetz reworked and resubmitted the bill to Ford, which now read: "$10.00 for tinkering around and $9,990 for knowing where to tinker."

Ford paid the bill.

EXPERTISE AND LEADERSHIP

THE PROBLEM

How to build strong employee relationships by using high-performance teams that will follow your leadership.

Putting together a group of experts with different, but complementary skills is the best way to form high-performance teams.

Goal-driven experts are attracted to those who also have expertise and will go to exceptional lengths to work with them. They understand that together they can create exciting and successful synergies that they would not be able to generate alone. In order to work with experts, most people will work harder, longer, and with more focus and dedication. They like the honor and status of working with those 'in the know'. They also like the intellectual growth that usually accompanies working in an expert environment.

STEPS

Step 1: Determine what expertise you require

Identify the areas of specialized expertise needed to accomplish your goals.

Step 2: Choose the team

Select people who have expertise in those specialized areas to be members of your team.

Step 3: Corral the breadth of knowledge

Require each team member to write a biography listing his/her background, training, experience, interests, skills, areas of expertise and accomplishments.

Step 4: Disseminate the information regarding your team members' expertise

- To build mutual respect, ensure that all team members are familiar with their teammates biographies, credentials, special skills and areas of expertise.
- Explain to team members precisely why you, as the team leader, chose each individual to be on the team.

Step 5: Explain every person's responsibility

Clearly explain to each team member his/her role and responsibility as well as the roles and responsibilities of all other team members. Inform each team member how his/her contribution fits with those of other team members and the objectives of the team and the company.

Step 6: Help your team bond and reach their full potential

- Give special awards to those who reach specific goals and publicly congratulate those who achieve success.

- Inform other team members of all significant developments in process because of the efforts of the team and/or its members.

- Keep your team informed of successes that team members have had on other teams, especially if your company has cross-functioning teams, on which team members are involved.

ALIGNMENT – RESPONSIBILITY, ACCOUNTABILITY, & AUTHORITY GUIDELINES

Defining the Formula for Success for Teams of Experts

In the movie, The Guns of Navarone, a diverse line up of experts was chosen to tackle a formidable task. Their goal was to disable the monstrous guns that sat high atop the cliffs protecting the Straights of Navarone. Allied ships could not sail through unless the goal was accomplished.

The team was successful for many reasons, however the most important reason was that the team members were clear about three vital components[1]:

Responsibility -- Each team member understood their team and personal responsibilities and tasks as they related to the goal. They discussed the requirements and expectations prior to accepting their assignments.

Accountability -- They were clear about how their team effort would be judged and how their individual efforts would be measured and deemed successful. The goal for defining authority guidelines is to marry expectations and metrics when deploying people. After the measurements of performance (accountability parameters) were reviewed, the parties agreed upon a set of metrics (quantifiable performance measurements). Each person knew the stakes and clearly grasped how others would determine whether they: a. met expectations, b. failed to deliver (needed improvement), or c. exceeded expectations and went above and beyond the call of duty.

---

[1] This is a brief summary of the process for defining responsibility, accountability, and authority guidelines described in the book *Alignment: The RA² Interface.*

Authority Guidelines -- All understood their authority as it pertained to their area of expertise and as it related to the other team members. A great leader knows that it is necessary to flow through the appropriate level of authority to individual team members so that they are able to accomplish their responsibilities without undue inefficiency, stress, or being forced to 'politic', 'beg', or 'grovel' for assistance from others. In the film, team members were clear about the team leader's level of authority and the team leader clearly communicated when he delegated authority to other team members. Clearly defined authority guidelines speed up goals and set people free to accomplish their objectives.

Several years ago, I was on a panel of six experts at Wharton Business School in Philadelphia. Of the six panel members, one was an economics professor who was the chair of his department and another was a wealthy real estate developer.

Halfway through the panel discussion, it was apparent that the economics professor was dominating the evening. The audience continually addressed him, soliciting opinions first about economics then about other topics. Time after time, he answered questions that clearly would have been better answered by another panel member. Many of his opinions were direct contradictions of the real estate developer's opinions.

Unfortunately, we did not have a moderator. I saw the panel members become increasingly uncomfortable. At the end of the evening, students surrounded the professor, vying for his attention. He reveled in their homage. From where I sat, it looked like he thought he had scored a homerun. Unfortunately for the professor, a reporter also attended the meeting. The next morning, the paper quoted the professor extensively in several areas out of his realm of expertise. Not once were the other panel members mentioned. The day after the article appeared, the real estate developer wrote a scathing rebuttal of the professor's opinions. Even worse, the rebuttal landed on the editor's desk.

Smelling a story, the editor told the reporter to dig deeper. The reporter had the tape of the event transcribed and he called the other panel members for their opinion about the professor's words. The next day, the paper ran a story that made the professor look like a fool. The other faculty members delighted in his downfall. Apparently this was typical behavior. The professor loved to hog the limelight. The good news was that the professor learned an important lesson. One week after the event, I picked up a voicemail apology from the professor. This was viewed as an excellent, open-minded gesture -- one that he repeated with every panel member – including the real estate developer.

 ## THE BOTTOM LINE

Make sure you are not acting in the role of an expert outside of your realm of expertise without thinking of the consequences. There are several lessons in this event. Clearly it would have been best for the audience had the professor allowed the appropriate expert answer questions from the audience. The professor, by not controlling his ego, did a professional disservice to his standing as an expert. He is an exceptionally bright man – a star in his field. Had he stuck to his area of expertise, the reporter would never have been able to fault him. There would not have been a scathing story. Fortunately, he was courageous enough (and smart enough) to apologize to everybody and in doing so recovered from an adverse situation. By handling this matter in an appropriate manner, he retained his expert status in his field. His written apology appeared in the paper with a compliment about his professional courtesy and conduct from the reporter.

What about his relationship with the real estate developer? The two initially chatted about the incident and since then have become good friends. However, the real estate developer confided that he still hasn't agreed to sit with the professor on a repeat performance of the infamous panel – no matter how many times the reporter has suggested it!

CHAPTER 9

THE LAW OF FRIENDS

People usually respond more favorably to advice and recommendations that they receive from friends. Most of us are more open to approaches made by friends because we believe they have our best interests at heart. Many people won't even consider referrals and recommendations that don't come from friends or close associates. The stronger the source of the referral, the weaker the resistance to influence.

Friends and family members whose opinions we value often provide the purest and most persuasive level of influence. Often, we willingly entertain new and even alien ideas simply because they are expressed by friends whom we respect. Similarly, we will often be more open to those who we previously shunned when our friends endorse them because we believe that our friends wish us nothing but the best. We value their opinion.

When you want to find a special restaurant, how do you go about it? Do you look in the paper to find an ad or do you ask a trusted friend whose taste and opinion you value? Have you ever received a phone call as you walked in the door from a stranger who says, "Hi, my name is so-and-so and I am with XYZ Company"? And, just as you are about to hang up, he adds, "Your friend Sam gave me your name." Suddenly, your irritation abates, you sigh, set your bag down, and start to listen.

We also invoke the Law of Friends when WE offer our recommendations, opinions and advice to our friends and family members. Our words have influence because of the depth and the quality of our relationships.

Even though we sometimes dislike what our friends and family members say, their influence still has tremendous sway in our thoughts and actions. An old English proverb says, *"Write down the advice of him who loves you, though you like it not at present."* Wise words!

 Beware!

Do not ask for favors based solely on your friendships as you run the risk of alienating your friends. At the least, you will make your friends uncomfortable. On the flip side, set appropriate limits with friends. If you are involved in a business relationship, clearly explain that you always make business decisions based on the merits of the facts. Stress that you want to help your friends become more successful, but be clear that they must be qualified and their requests must have merit.

When you are in a position of authority, consider other peoples' perception of your motives. Will they think you are 'playing favorites'? If they might, ask yourself: "Am I?" If you hope to be a successful leader, avoid any appearance of favoritism because it can undermine your authority.

The advice of friends must be received with a judicious reserve; we must not give ourselves up to it and follow it blindly, whether right or wrong.

Pierre Charron

INFLUENCE ILLUSTRATED

Benjamin Franklin is one of the most revered figures in American history, but he was not always well liked. In his autobiography, Franklin even described himself as unattractive and uncouth. He decided to change when a long time friend told him, "Ben, you are impossible. You have no tact and your opinions demean those who disagree with you. In fact, people find that they enjoy themselves better when you are not around!"

Although the criticism hurt, Franklin was confident that his friend's advice was sincere and he took its message to heart. Over time, Franklin dramatically altered his persona and he is now remembered as one of our most popular and well-loved founding fathers.

Friends in your life are like pillars on your porch. Sometimes they hold you up, and sometimes they lean on you. Sometimes it's just enough to know that they're standing by in case the weather changes.

Anonymous

 THE PROBLEM

My firm, Indaba was asked to help an executive team select a leader for a multimillion-dollar project. The executive team realized that the selection of the appropriate leader would very much determine whether people would work cooperatively together. This in turn would govern how smoothly the project would run; whether the deliverables were discharged on time and within the scope of the budget.

STEPS

Step 1: Examine the candidates

First we reviewed the resumes of four candidates. Two we dismissed immediately: one for lacking technical expertise and the second because he couldn't be spared from a critical project that he was handling for another customer.

Step 2: Weigh the hard and soft skills

We examined the qualifications of the two remaining candidates. Of the two, Stephen had far better technical skills and ten years more experience than Marjorie. On the other hand, Marjorie understood the importance of the Law of Friends and had friends throughout the company. She also had a knack for cultivating friends at different levels of authority. She not only forged relationships with co-workers but with people in positions of influence within the corporation as well as several highly placed mentors outside the company.

Step 3: Question your choices

In discussing the candidates, a team member immediately questioned Stephen's ability to lead the project by saying, "I know he's good technically, but my people will have a problem with him. On his last team, he quickly made enemies and, to make matters worse, he didn't make enough friends to help him with those who disliked him. I don't know of anybody in my department who would be overjoyed to work with him, even though they all realize he's very sharp and knows his stuff."

A second team member added that Stephen had a reputation for team breaking, not team building and that he had not made many friends. In fact, he pointed out that people might even subtly try to sabotage him and they certainly would not go the extra mile for him. Marjorie however, he stressed, had made plenty of friends. Everybody loved her. Even when she has something unpleasant to say, she says it respectfully. As a result, people listen and tend to follow her. He also recommended that Marjorie lead the project rather than Stephen.

Step 4: Do your homework

I did some investigative work and talked with people who were at all levels of the corporation about Marjorie. Shortly thereafter, Marjorie asked me to lunch. When she invited me, she said that she had heard that I was asking questions about her and would I mind speaking with her directly?

As soon as we sat down, I said, "I think you have a bright future with the corporation. Do you realize what a great job you do making friends?" I mentioned that several executives had praised her and that I was intrigued since executives rarely speak so highly of a manager. I explained that's why I decided to ask around to find out more about her.

Marjorie replied that she thought making friends was one of her greatest strengths. She recognized that her ability to make friends at the executive level had helped her and she correctly guessed which executives had spoken up in her favor. How clever! I guess Marjorie knew that it always helps to have friends in high places. Good for her!

 THE BOTTOM LINE

Marjorie received the promotion and did a fine job. Luckily for Stephen, the executive team recognized his value to the organization and he also had some supporters. Because of his loyal service they wanted him to succeed so they arranged for Indaba to counsel him on the importance of building relationships and establishing friendships with his co-workers and peers.

To Stephen's credit, he had taken well to the one-on-one coaching. The next step -- it was time to actively work at turning around his prickly reputation. However, I had to do this fast so that Stephen was not passed over again for the next big project. Stephen had to make friends in a hurry at all levels of the corporation. Our tactic was for him to start a ping-pong club twice a week after work. Soon the club was so successful that Stephen convinced the company to purchase three more tables. Now they had four rollaway tables which Stephen and some of the other employees quickly set up straight after work on Tuesday and Thursday evenings. Within a short period, Stephen started to be known as a fun guy!

Word spread that he was the go-to guy for getting things accomplished. He had started the club, organized funding for new tables and supplies, and he even procured food and drinks for a nominal fee. The word was that he even had the executive team pony up some prizes for the championships. What a cool guy! His friendly ping-pong reputation quickly jumped over to his business relationships. Because of the table tennis evenings, Stephen started to make friends across the company at all levels.

Later that same year when it was time to decide on a new leader for another important program, Stephen had lots of people willing to work with him. In fact, the biggest surprise to the executive team was that one of Stephen's biggest cheerleaders was Josh, a manager who had refused point blank to work with him six months prior. When I spoke to that manager, he even admitted that he liked Stephen now and had even invited him and his family over for a barbeque. Stephen laughed and said they turned out to be friends because he let Josh beat him a couple of times at ping-pong.

As I write this, Stephen is being considered for a substantial promotion when his boss retires in six months. Right now, the way I see it, there is no doubt that he'll get it. Who says you can't teach an old dog new tricks?

CHAPTER 10

THE LAW OF IMAGE

People are more likely to interact with people they are attracted to and who have an appropriate appearance for the setting or situation. Whether philosophically you agree or disagree that image should matter is irrelevant. The question is: Does image influence how other people judge us? The answer is a resounding "yes". People judge us -- positively or negatively -- based on their perception of the appropriateness of our image as it relates to the occasion and as it relates to them personally. This is a biased gut-felt reaction and can be inappropriately prejudiced.

How others perceive you is a vital part of the influencing process. Right or wrong, people are simply attracted to those who look good to them: physically, intellectually, spiritually, and in virtually every other way. As shallow as it may seem, it's an instinctive thing; people simply feel more comfortable with those they find attractive.

The Law of Image holds that when people believe you have a terrific image, they will be more subject to your influence. They will want to be with you, be seen with you, emulate you, imitate you, and follow your leadership. Conversely, they will not respond positively to those whose image doesn't feel right. Do you really want your banker or financial professional to conduct a business meeting unshaven, dressed in jeans and a T-shirt? How would you feel if they did? The bottom line is that the appropriate image creates the appropriate level of trust.

The Law of Image is easy to apply. Learn what others expect of you and influence them by complying with their expectations. Simply put, the goal is to fit into their ideal image.

 Beware!

Dress appropriately. Impressions count. Appearance also extends to business materials, cars, business locations, and other manifestations of image.

Ask yourself if you are being influenced because people's ideas are sound or because they look good or their offices are beautiful? Be wary of giving your business to firms that look good unless you check behind the veneer. Always scratch beneath the surface.

A friend left a well-paid job to join a firm that went bankrupt within eight weeks. She knew she would quit her job the minute she saw the plush oriental carpets and expensive leather that adorned the reception area. The beautifully dressed receptionist who served her water in a tall crystal glass also awed her. "Imagine working here!" she thought as she waited for her interview.

The interview started promptly and she was ushered into a fabulous office. A tall, handsome, silver-haired executive stood waiting patiently. After fifteen minutes, her interviewer said the job was hers and asked if she liked the office they were sitting in. He told her it would be hers if she made the decision to join today. They were ramping up so fast they needed an answer quickly, he claimed, and although two other candidates were willing to commit and start immediately, they really wanted her. Although she knew better, because she hadn't yet researched the corporation's financials, she immediately said "yes!"

In fact, the company was in deep financial difficulty. They wanted her because she had an excellent financial reputation, was stable, conservative and was known in the business community not to take risks. To compound matters, her immediate resignation from her current position caused irreparable damage to her professional reputation.

So don't get blinded by looks or overwhelmed by the whirlwind of a well-orchestrated Law of Image influencing strategy. Look past the glitter. Find the substance and make sure appearances don't deceive you or lower your guard against undue influence.

Studies show that the first person to be hired in a company is the one **most** like the boss and the first one that will be terminated is the one **least** like the boss.

Harvard Business Journal

INFLUENCE ILLUSTRATED

During a televised debate between Ronald Reagan and Walter Mondale in the 1984 Presidential Campaign, the issue of Reagan's age came up – despite the fact that he had just served as the nation's president for four years.

When a reporter asked if he was "too old to serve another term", Reagan was prepared and his response put his critics to silence. "I'm not going to inject the issue of age into this campaign. I am not going to exploit for political gain my opponent's youth and inexperience," was Reagan's fabulous retort.

 THE PROBLEM

A large East Coast electrical utility asked me to coach Jennifer, a high-potential manager, because her staff was not performing up to par. Since she took charge, deadlines slipped and grievances were up. Fortunately, none of them were directed at Jennifer and most targeted other team members.

STEPS

Step 1: Solicit advice

I interviewed the Vice President of Human Relations who thought that Jennifer's choice of business attire could be a factor. In her last position, as the manager of customer liaison, Jennifer wore a uniform -- blue pants and a button-down shirt with a company logo.

Step 2: Uncover the issue

I met with Jennifer who told me, "I just don't think my employees are taking me seriously. For example, I spoke to their old manager about the department's high absenteeism and he said that he never had a problem. I gave him figures that showed a sharp increase."

Jennifer also consulted her predecessor regarding the disrespect team members were exhibiting toward one another. He said that he had that problem in the beginning of his tenure but quickly nipped it in the bud. Jennifer continued, "Although I've told them that I expect them to treat each other respectfully, they just don't seem to listen. The same thing with accountability; when I discuss deadlines, I might as well be talking to the wall! I'm at my wits end!"

Jennifer, a pretty brunette, was about 5'2' tall and 150 pounds. She had been trying -- unsuccessfully -- to knock off 30 pounds that she had been carrying since the birth of her last child. When we met, she was dressed in an over-sized brightly colored, baggy sweater that had seen better days. The sleeves, which were way too long, were rolled up and pushed close to her elbows. Jennifer also wore black stretch pants and sneakers. No wonder her team wasn't listening – who would take her seriously and respect her as a manager dressed like that?

Step 3: Address the issue openly

In my most tactful manner, taking great pains not to offend her, I explained to Jennifer that I thought she had to upgrade her wardrobe. To command the respect required to get her job done, she needed to look more like a manager. Jennifer protested saying that she didn't own much business clothing. She stated that she was trying to lose weight, was going to a gym regularly and didn't have the money to "buy a wardrobe that won't fit in a few months". After she finished, I stressed that dressing the part of a manager was vital to her success. Ultimately, she agreed.

Step 4: Plan to change

We needed a plan. If we shocked the staff by suddenly and dramatically changing Jennifer's attire over night, it could backfire. It also might look like upper level management had told her to change. Although this was somewhat true, we wanted to keep this issue confidential. So we decided to implement a gradual transition of her wardrobe over the next several weeks.

Step 5: Command the resources

I explained the financial dilemma to the VP of HR. She procured $350 from the utility to help Jennifer start dressing like a manager. Then I took her to a friend's upscale consignment store after work to build a basic manager's wardrobe: a couple of jackets, three skirts and blouses, two pairs of pants, a couple of pairs of professional shoes, and a cardigan.

Step 6: Implement the plan

I instructed Jennifer to wear a skirt and jacket on days when she held staff meetings. I advised her to schedule appointments with customers on staff meeting days so her team didn't think that she was dressing up just for them. Then I recommended that she should start gradually upgrading her wardrobe until she dressed like a manager every day.

I also suggested that she implement an agenda at meetings to stress to her staff that she was serious about holding them accountable for deadlines. We also rehearsed specific wording she would use when informing her group about her expectations on absenteeism and respect between employees.

THE BOTTOM LINE

Within six weeks, Jennifer's team dramatically changed. Absenteeism stabilized to normal levels almost overnight. Team members treated each other more respectfully during meetings.

The best news was that Jennifer noticed changes in her staff members' body language when she spoke to them. They took her seriously, listened, and showed respect for her expectations. About four months later, I received a strange package. It contained the baggy, brightly colored sweater with a note that said, "I can't believe I actually wore this to the office! Can you? Thanks! Jennifer"

CHAPTER 11

THE LAW OF LOGIC

People are more subject to influence when they can follow a sequence of thoughts that make sense to them. Logic and clarity are essential to the influencing process because when people are confused they usually refuse to take action.

To influence others, the point you are trying to make must make good sense to them. The person you are trying to persuade must be able to follow a logical sequence of reasons that lead to a conclusion they can embrace. You can influence decisions even more effectively if you combine logic with a sense of urgency. Logical reasons must be advanced that will validate their decision to follow your direction (influencing path).

 **Beware!**

When others are attempting to influence you, check the logic of their arguments. Make sure you base your decisions on the facts, not just on their opinions.

Even the world's best companies have been known to make errors. Always ask, "Does this make sense?" Check your facts and trust your intuition before committing valuable time, energy, and resources.

A lapse in logic might:
- ➢ Destroy trust
- ➢ Negatively impact rapport
- ➢ Damage credibility
- ➢ Make you look unprepared, uninformed and/or unprofessional.

> I know you believe you understand what you think I said, but I am not sure you realize that what you heard is not what I meant.
>
> **Anonymous**

INFLUENCE ILLUSTRATED

An Irish peasant woman taught a valuable lesson to Ralph Waldo Emerson, the great historian, noted poet, and respected philosopher. Emerson and his son were attempting to get a calf into their barn, but their pushing and pulling had no effect on the heifer, which stubbornly refused to move. The woman, who was passing by, saw their predicament and asked if she could help. Sarcastically, Emerson replied that she could "if she thought she could do anything." The woman then thrust her fingers in the calf's mouth and within moments had it following her into the barn. As a result, Emerson wrote in his journal that evening:

People possess some comparable characteristics displayed by the young calf. You can push them, pull them, prod them, or even kick them, and they won't move, but give them a reason they can understand, one that will prove beneficial to them, and they will follow peacefully along. People don't do things because you want them to. They perform a certain way because they want to. When I learn what is important to others, it makes working with them simpler.

 THE PROBLEM

Bruce's boss was out of his depth with making a technical decision that would negatively affect Bruce's project. Bruce had to bring his boss up to speed and influence his thinking without making a career-limiting move!

STEPS

Step 1: Define the issue and determine the goal

If you don't start by identifying your objective, you run the risk of waffling or going off track, which will prevent you from clearly focusing on your target. Lack of focus will delay your progress, which will irritate your boss. To avoid unnecessary detours, Bruce asked, "What exactly do I hope to achieve? What are my precise goals? What is the fundamental issue? What solution must result?" He then tried to visualize how the perfect solution would look.

Step 2: Uncover the reasons for their views

Bruce then tried to understand his boss' thinking. He asked these questions:
- How did his boss actually formulate his beliefs?
- What is the basis for his boss' current knowledge and position?
- Does he lack the knowledge needed to make the right decision? If so, what specific information does he need to bring him up to speed?
- Is his current knowledge reality-based? If the boss lacked sufficient knowledge, would he be open to Bruce's input or suggestions from other people (if so, who specifically would he listen to)?

Step 3: Set the context

The closer Bruce got to the center of the bull's eye, the more emotional involvement he saw from his boss. The further away from the center, the less motivated his boss appeared. Bruce imagined the bull's eye as his boss (as he saw himself), the next ring as the team, then the department, the division, the region, the company, the industry, the world and the universe. Bruce knew if he wanted his boss to get emotional and personally involved, he had to set the stage for him to be in the middle of the consequences. If he wanted his boss to make an unemotional decision, he had to set the context as a corporate profit item – not one that directly impacted the boss' year-end bonus.

Step 4: Put together logical counter points

Next, Bruce identified all current and potential objections as he went through the influencing process. He asked how he could convince his boss to alter his thinking? What proof could he provide to refute what his boss currently believed to be true? Could he provide irrefutable cause and effect relationships to back up his position?

Step 5: Define the short and long term ramifications

The consequences of choosing one approach over another were then examined. Bruce steered his boss toward his position and away from opposing views. To do so he relied on the fact that people tend to move easily toward pleasure and away from pain. So, he structured his arguments to clearly define the pleasure (positive consequences of going along with him) as well as defining the pain (negative consequences) that could arise under other approaches.

Step 6: Close decisively

Finally, Bruce explained, on the basis of the logic he outlined, why his alternative was the wisest course of action. Bruce kept it simple by sealing his explanation with a KISS – Keep It Simple, Stupid!

☀ THE BOTTOM LINE

His boss was wowed by Bruce's presentation. Bruce reported that he actually said, "That's the most logical presentation I've ever seen. Let's go ahead and put some numbers together. Meet with the Director of Communications to see what we would need to tell the customers and our sales people. I'd like you to show them this presentation and get their input, but I can't see them giving us any objections based on what you showed me today. It just makes perfect sense!"

Six months later, Bruce's boss was commended for his foresight in launching the new product enhancements He received a promotion and a substantial bonus. The CEO was especially thrilled since the original technology plan was based on a platform that had since become an industry dinosaur. Bruce's boss' decision saved the company more than $350,000. Bruce received a large bonus and was promoted to VP of Information Services. What a logical choice!

CHAPTER 12

THE LAW OF PEOPLE PLEASING

To influence others, identify what will please them and deliver it to them. Be gracious and generous, not only with close friends and those you hold dear, but also with others less familiar. It's a marvelous way to make new friends and valuable contacts. Continually try to find what gives people pleasure and then try to provide it.

Bend over backwards to ensure that those you try to please never feel obligated to you or feel the need to reciprocate. The best way to do so is by giving on an emotional level. For example, convey warm feelings and perform helpful acts rather than give material gifts, which often carry implied obligations and can create the impression that you're angling for something in return. When used at its ultimate, the Law of People Pleasing simply lets others know that you are thinking of them, that you wish them well, or want to help them succeed.

Before attempting to please others, verify what they truly value or need. Find out what is important to them, learn what they need, and identify how you can help them. Often, well-meaning givers act on the basis of what they think others want and they often get it wrong. So check your information to confirm that your instincts are on target.

NOTE: If someone you try to please INSISTS on reciprocating, allow the person to do so only if you were clear that you had no expectation or desire for anything in return. Keep in mind that some people simply cannot accept a gift without giving one in return. In those cases, it would be ungracious not to let them do what they consider appropriate. See also Chapter 15, the Law of Reciprocity.

Beware!

Respect is a vital element in the Law of Pleasing People. Become sensitive to what *pleases and displeases* other people. Observe their reactions.

Indaba was brought in to smooth over a cultural issue that offended several of a client's employees who were born in India. The client believed in educating employees and was impressed by a program entitled 'Sacred Cows Make the Best Burgers' so he ordered all employees to attend a seminar based on the program.

Personally, I liked the book, video, ideas, and materials in the course. I especially liked the humorous way the author broached his subject matter. But having grown up in Africa on the Indian Ocean, I realized immediately why the employees from India were upset. Since my client had several employees from India, the program was not appropriate for his workforce. Luckily, my client withdrew the mandate immediately and issued a sincere apology in writing and by email. At my suggestion, he sent a voicemail apology to all employees and at the annual meeting, he allowed the employees to perform a light-hearted parody about his insensitivity and laughed along with them as he was 'enlightened' by a woman in traditional Indian garb and an actor dressed like Gandhi.

> If you will please people, you must please them in their own way; and as you cannot make them what they should be, you must take them as they are.
>
> **Lord Chesterfield**

INFLUENCE ILLUSTRATED

During the Civil War, Abraham Lincoln often visited hospitals to talk to the wounded. At one visit, he came upon a young soldier who was near death. Lincoln asked the soldier if there was anything he could do. Unaware that he was speaking with the President, the soldier asked Lincoln to write a letter to his mother, which he then dictated to the President.

The letter read, "My Dearest Mother, I was badly hurt while doing my duty. I'm afraid that I am not going to recover. Don't grieve too much for me, please. Kiss Mary and John for me. May God bless you and Father." Lincoln signed the young man's name for him and added a postscript "Written for your son by Abraham Lincoln".

When the soldier read the note, he was astonished to discover that it had been written by the President. "Are you really the President?" he asked in awe. Lincoln said, "Yes" and asked if he could do anything more.

Weakly the soldier nodded, "Please hold my hand. I think it would help to see me through to the end." Lincoln complied and stayed with him until dawn, offering empathy and compassion until the morning when death came and took the young soldier.

 ## THE PROBLEM

How can you get the people you deal with to give you their maximum effort?

STEPS

Step 1: Give warranted praise

Look for opportunities to praise people and commend them when they make a significant effort. Extol them when they go that extra mile. Mean what you say and never give praise when it's not warranted. False praise will kill your credibility.

Step 2: Be sensitive to diversity and cultural issues

Show interest in differences and consider them opportunities for you to learn. What you discover can broaden your thinking and expose you to new opportunities and rewards.

Step 3: Learn what matters to people

Remember significant details about family and interests. If you can't remember, write it down where it will be easily accessible. Be able to answer the following questions:

- What schools do their children attend? (People LOVE to talk about their children!)
- What are their hobbies?
- What other projects is he/she involved in?
- Is he/she contributing to the community on behalf of your company? If so, in what way?
- Is he/she mentoring other employees? If so, how is the program going? Discuss the results and thank the individual for their time.

- When is the person's birthday?
- What is the name of their spouse?
- What are the names of their children?
- How old are his/her children?
- What are their talents?

Step 4: Recognize significant achievements

Has the employee recently been issued a patent, won any awards, come up with any innovative ideas or approaches or experienced any major events such as marriage, a birth, a new home? If so, send them a congratulatory note, voicemail or recognize them during a meeting. Also express your sympathies when family members pass away or are going through a health crisis.

Step 5: Listen and encourage

Listen to employees when they have difficult times and encourage them. Follow up with supportive notes, emails or voicemail.

Step 6: Think of the appropriate reward

Be flexible when giving prizes and awards. Think about what that particular person would like. Be creative, thoughtful and generous in your choice.

Step 7: Remember significant events

Send anniversary letters to employees commemorating their tenure with the company and mention significant milestones in your newsletter or other company communications.

Step 8: Remember the family

When someone's efforts have taken substantially from his/her family time, send a gift certificate to their spouse, or buy circus or movies tickets for the family. Although these small gifts won't give them back the time lost with their family, it will show that you recognize and appreciate their sacrifice, which will build goodwill.

Step 9: Wish people well

Send flowers, a get-well card, or a gift basket to the hospital or home if your employee, their spouse or children are ill.

 ## THE BOTTOM LINE

Get in the habit of making affirmative gestures that show you care. Always clearly express your appreciation. Create and implement a company-wide program that will foster appreciation and good will. Make it a practice to continually give of yourself.

CHAPTER 13

THE LAW OF PERCEPTION

Our opinions and responses to influence are based on our personal experiences, beliefs, values and perspectives. Yet, our <u>instinctive</u> reactions seldom take into account the other person's perspectives. It's easier to exert influence when everyone is working within the same framework and wants to achieve the same goals. However, this isn't always possible or even realistic when people are trying to influence each other to achieve their individual – and often divergent -- goals. If you can uncover and understand how the other person perceives the world, you can plug your influencing strategy into their perception of what is happening. Do this on a consistent basis and you will be ahead of the pack.

Master influencers manage both their own and other people's perceptions. They know that we all see things from different perspectives. Therefore, they strive to understand the other person's viewpoint so that they can present their arguments in terms that others can easily understand.

If you adamantly try to convince someone of equal power to accept your beliefs without presenting your opinions and viewpoints *from their perspective*, you're heading for disaster. If you hope to work successfully with people you've convinced, it's more likely that you'll succeed when they can see the benefits in their terms. Otherwise, there may be a residue of lingering doubt and resentment that can come back to haunt you.

Be smart. Create partnerships, not domination.

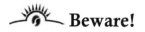 **Beware!**

Sam Walton, the founder of Wal-Mart and Sam's Club, was washing his old pickup outside his store when two executives in expensive suits drove up. These gentlemen were hoping to do business with Wal-Mart and had an appointment to meet Mr. Walton that morning. They thought it would be nice to greet him as he arrived. Unfortunately, neither executive knew what Sam Walton looked like. They looked toward Sam washing his old pickup truck, but ignored him. When better-dressed (read: management type) Wal-Mart employees arrived for work, the visitors asked them, "When does Sam Walton typically arrive at his office?"

"What a strange question," the manager thought as they looked past the visitors and saw their employer washing his car not twenty feet away. Sam Walton acknowledged their surprise and with a big knowing wink. The employee got the picture and answered, "Oh, he usually gets up to his office about 9:00 after he walks around the store for a while." The visitors asked, "Where does he usually park?" "Over there," the manager answered as they gestured to Sam and the pickup. For the next thirty minutes, the visitors questioned many employees as they arrived for work, "Is he in the store yet?" "No, not yet," they answered when they saw Sam wink. It was obvious to Mr. Walton and his employees that the visitors were hoping to meet him before he went inside.

Minutes before 9 o'clock, the visitors went inside. Sam finished, parked his pickup, and headed up to his office. Imagine the visitors' surprise when they met Sam Walton. When Sam escorted the visitors to their car, he made it clear that he did business with people who understood his business philosophy. "All Wal-Mart stores", he explained, "have employees who greet every person who enters our store. We have this policy because it is important to be polite and speak to everybody – no matter what they drive, what they look like, and what you think of them." That was how Sam Walton did business and he chose vendors who understood his philosophy and lived by it.

To get others to do what you want them to do, you must see things through their eyes.

David J. Schwartz

INFLUENCE ILLUSTRATED

A man in China raised horses for a living. One day, one of his prized stallions ran away. His friends gathered at his home to mourn his loss.

The next week, the runaway horse returned with several strays following close behind. The same acquaintances again assembled at his home, but this time to celebrate his good fortune.

That afternoon the horse kicked his owner's son and broke his back. Once more, the crowd came to express their sorrow for the son's injury.

However, in the next month, war broke out and the son was exempted from ten years of military service because of his broken back.

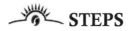 THE PROBLEM

An outside Board Member and the corporation's CEO were at loggerheads about how the organization should be restructured. Communication had shut down and each refused to listen to the other. Our goal: Get them to understand each other's position, communicate appropriately, restructure the company in a timely manner, and most important, shake hands and move forward without holding grudges.

STEPS

Step 1: Examine the opposing parties' beliefs

The CEO, who had an engineering background, saw the restructuring project as strictly a management issue. He felt that the Board Member was overstepping his authority by insisting that he participate in the development of the restructuring plan.

The Board Member's experience was in the retail industry on the opposite coast. He believed that the corporation's 'annual restructurings' had negative consequences on the company's profits and personnel. In the last restructuring, which was just nine months before, several key employees left because they were unhappy with their reassignments. Whenever profits were impacted, he insisted, the Board had a fiduciary responsibility to step in and monitor the situation.

Step 2: Assess the problem objectively

In most disputes, I try to get the disputing parties to meet face-to-face to sort out their differences. By the time I was called in, the two had been jockeying for position and lobbying other Board Members, customers, and corporate executives for support for weeks. Their spat was having a disruptive affect throughout the corporation. This was not the first time the two had stubbornly refused to communicate. I swiftly concluded that they were not capable of communicating effectively without the intervention of an outside facilitator.

Step 3: Define the objectives

I was brought in to:
i.   Explain to the combatants the negative consequences of their failure to communicate
ii. Stop a pattern of negative communication
iii. Convey guidelines for positive communication
iv. Reestablish the basis for their business relationship and
v.   Make sure that they continued to communicate in the future.

Step 4: Communicate the ground rules for the meeting

I arranged for the three of us to meet. When the meeting opened, I explained the guidelines and stressed that I was in charge of running this meeting. I clarified that my goals were to get them to communicate now and lay the groundwork for them to effectively communicate in the future. In addition, I let them know that I had researched their positions and interviewed many people who were familiar with the situation. These opening remarks set the tone and fortunately, at this point, both were quiet and willing to listen.

Step 5: Define the process for moving forward

Each would have the opportunity to voice their opinions without interruption, I explained. I suggested that they each listen with an open mind and, after each had stated his position, I would put forth my conclusions on:
a) What caused their communication breakdown?
b) The steps for them to immediately move forward and communicate.
c) A process to improve their future working relationship.
d) A plan to demonstrate to others who had observed their problems that they could work together without rancor.

Step 6: Get agreement and set deadlines

I emphasized the importance of their working out their problems as quickly as possible. They agreed to remain in the meeting until they had decided if and when a restructuring should in fact occur. And, if they decided to move forward, when the reorganization should take place.

The Board Member said that restructuring during the stressful annual review process exacerbated the negative effects of the prior reorganization plans. The CEO agreed to be more thoughtful about his timing and to solicit (and listen to) input from Board Members. When the Board Member asked why the CEO felt it necessary to restructure now and couldn't wait at least six months, the CEO explained his reasoning. He admitted making a mistake with the last reorganization plan. The Board Member understood, accepted, and agreed to support his decision.

To avoid or at least minimize past mistakes, they decided to establish clear guidelines to measure the success or failure of the current restructuring and other initiatives. They also agreed that the Board and the executive team would be involved in determining the timing of major initiatives, but the Board Member agreed that the final decision about restructuring rested with the CEO. However, I could easily tell that the Board Member still did not think that a total reorganization was the answer. I also knew that the CEO understood that it was highly disruptive.

Step 7: Saving face

The Board Member understood how difficult it was for the CEO to admit making a mistake to a Board Member. He had been in a similar position and offered valuable insight on how he had recovered. Both men knew that what was said in the meeting was confidential and must remain in that room; trust was imperative. Their compromise was a clear message that they were willing to abandon their stubborn positions and help each other save face. **Remember:** Whenever you 'win', always find ways to let your opponent save face. It's a proven, and wise way to avoid bitterness and move forward productively.

☀ THE BOTTOM LINE

By sitting down together and listening openly, two powerful men began to understand each other's perspective. Each gained insight into how the other viewed his roles and responsibilities. Prior to the meeting, each took an all-or-nothing approach, but once they started listening, I quickly realized that it might be time to suggest a compromise. I waited, picked my moment, and asked if a partial restructuring might be the possible. The timing of my words was good. Immediately, I noticed both men smile.

After a few points were ironed out, they agreed to a partial restructuring that would take place over three months. I pointed out that the executive team should solicit input from Board Members, which made the Board Member happy. The Board Member agreed to give management final authority on restructuring initiatives, which placated the CEO. All agreed that attrition caused by restructuring would be monitored, its impact analyzed, and that management would create and give the Board a plan to retain key people who might be impacted.

I was invited to attend the next board meeting and was delighted to see how productively the CEO and Board Member cooperated. They outlined their agreement, sought input from the others at the table, and moved forward as if their problem was a non-issue. Better yet, they joked with each other and when two problems arose, they discussed them respectfully and quickly worked them out.

I frequently see the former adversaries and am happy to report that they have not reverted to their old destructive, negative behavior. In fact, I consider them role models for how a Board Member and the head of a corporation's executive team should interact.

CHAPTER 14

THE LAW OF PROSPECTING AND NETWORKING

People are more likely to succeed when they receive help from those who have the resources and/or contacts to help them reach their goals. Goal-setters understand that their objectives can be more quickly met when their circle of friends and acquaintances are involved. The more your network is in tune with your dreams, the stronger your chances of success.

It's hard to do it by yourself. To succeed in today's complex world, it takes teamwork. Even if you're the world's leading expert, many obstacles exist and it invariably takes more than just what you know to get everything done.

To make it today, you must know and get help from people who know what you don't. And they must know and be willing to send you to others who know even more and agree to share their information and contacts with you. The more widely and diversely you can extend your circle, the better your chances of success.

The trick is to become a connector! In our self-obsessed world, most people have the dial stuck on WIIFM (What's In It For Me?) They always ask, "Who has the ability to help me achieve my goals?"

Distinguish yourself by becoming a connector. As a connector you can help others make important contacts, who will help them succeed. If you help enough people, frequently enough, they, in turn, will help you by connecting you to others who can fulfill your needs faster than you ever could have done yourself.

Be patient! Mastering the Law of Prospecting and Networking does not happen overnight. You must plant seeds that will subsequently bear fruit. If you haven't started to sharpen your prospecting skills and cultivating your network contacts, **get moving**. Start building a network of contacts who have diverse abilities, backgrounds, and expertise **today**. Find people who can support your talents and fill in your gaps. Then create an influencing plan that will position you to achieve your goals.

Beef up your contact database and make it a point to stay in touch with them. Keep detailed records so that you can call on your network when you need them. Then you too can be known as a networker and prospector extraordinaire.

Be prepared and willing to act when someone in your network calls you. How can you expect assistance when you are not prepared and willing to assist others? For example, if your business depends on referrals for its success, get comfortable with giving out referrals. What goes around, comes around.

Beware!

Prospecting and networking strategies are more art than science. It takes more finesse to become an influential networker than simply collecting names and contacts. It takes sensitivity, consideration, and a sense of what is appropriate, which many people lack. For example, the following story actually occurred.

I was working with a client who was having problems prospecting. He never seemed to know what to do. Repeatedly, he would ask me, "When is the best time to prospect? Is it all right the first time I meet someone? Is it better after I get the sale? Even if I don't make the sale, are you telling me it's okay to ask for names?" After several months of these and similar questions, I was starting to get a little frustrated. I finally said, "Listen, prospecting and networking happen everywhere. It's so ingrained that I just do it all the time."

Unfortunately, he took my words literally. A couple of days later he couldn't wait to say to me, "You'll be SO proud of me. I actually got two referrals this weekend at a funeral. You were right, you can prospect anywhere!" What can I say? Nothing, except that this type of ill-mannered networking unfortunately happens too often.

Use common sense! Be diplomatic and be sensitive. Be in tune with the event and your surroundings, the people's moods, and with their willingness to refer you to others.

My research offers impressive evidence that we feel better when we attempt to make our world better… to have a purpose beyond one's self lends to existence a meaning and direction – the most important characteristic of high well-being.

Gail Sheehy

INFLUENCE ILLUSTRATED

This is a parable about two seas in Palestine. One sea is a living sea; it has fresh water and is home to fish, children play in it, and nature grows on its banks. The River Jordan flows into the fresh-water sea filling it with sparkling water from the hills.

However, the Jordan also runs into another sea: a stale, dank body without trees, shrubs, fish, or people around it. Nothing lives in this sea so it's called the Dead Sea. The Dead Sea hoards all the water that it receives and gives nothing back.

The living sea, on the other hand, gives back each drop of water it receives. The reason it is so bountiful is because the cycle of life keeps it alive. It gives freely of its water and, in return, plants and animals give back precious organic matter to balance the sea's mineral levels enabling marine life to exist. What goes around comes around in the cycle of life. The bountiful sea reaches out to help others to thrive and as a result, it thrives itself.

PROSPECTING AND NETWORKING AND LEADERSHIP

 ## THE PROBLEM

Due to a merger, a large part of a telecommunications giant's Customer Service Department was being moved out of state. The move was nine months down the road. Indaba was hired to boost morale and teach employees how to deal with the upcoming changes. On this assignment, we worked directly with the Director of Customer Service who clearly demonstrated his brilliance in prospecting and networking.

STEPS

Step 1: First decisions, fast decisions

The Director searched for and identified employees from all company departments who wanted to move to the new location. This allowed him to quickly fill a number of positions with a base of willing transferees, which alleviated some of the initial pressure of the move. Be decisive early on when change is forced upon you. It gives people hope during turbulent times. During a storm, the captain cannot stand idly by. He must quickly take charge, take action, and take control of the situation. Action lowers stress and creates momentum.

Step 2: Work the phones

To place his current employees, the Director worked the phones and networked. He identified each employee's assets and skills, and matched them with the talents needed for the new jobs. When he called his contacts, both in and outside of the company, he gave them the opportunity to hire wonderful, loyal employees, which can be an exceptional gift!

100

Step 3: The ability to handle simultaneous, seemingly contradictory tasks is the mark of a true leader

The Director then contacted a variety of local associations, including Chambers of Commerce, to find additional candidates who would be open to jobs at the new location. Combined with his other moves, this enabled him to cover a significant portion of the new site's staffing before the move occurred. I think that the difference between a leader and a manager is the ability to work with simultaneous, seemingly contradictory tasks and to effectively handle paradoxical situations and decisions.

Step 4: Implement and integrate

The Director called upon his network to help integrate the new employees into the new location. First, he contacted company managers and other personnel who had benefited by getting good people in the move. He also appealed to employees he helped place in new jobs. He asked them for names of people they knew in the new location who could ease the transition so the newcomers would be happier and more productive. When the Director called for assistance, <u>it was provided because he had previously helped his contacts.</u>

Step 5: Open door, open communication

He instituted an open-door policy to encourage current employees to stop by his office. When they showed up, which most did, he interviewed them to learn what they would accept and reject with regard to transfers and positions with other companies, which made placements easier.

Step 6: Ask for help when you need it

When employees visited his office, the Director made calls to get help placing workers in other jobs. He realized that most employees preferred not to relocate. He also understood that an unwillingness to relocate did not mean that the employee was disloyal to the company. To help his people, he was not afraid to call in favors with contacts at his company and in other industries.

☼ THE BOTTOM LINE

The Director placed all his employees from the old location. In three months, he helped place 175 employees in new positions with his company; 78 others moved to new jobs with other companies with his assistance, and 47 moved to the new location.

Because of the Director's efforts, most employees left for new positions ahead of schedule and the relocation moved forward by three months. This saved the company $550,000 and it realized further savings of nearly $750,000 because the corporation did not have to pay severance payments or outplacement fees.

For his accomplishments, the Director was promoted and put in charge of customer service for the entire business division, including expansion at the new location. He was charged with hiring and training 250 new employees in six months. By working the phones, he arranged for the department to be fully staffed and running in three months. In doing so, he paid no headhunting fees and placed no newspaper advertisements. The Law of Prospecting and Networking pays fabulous dividends when you know what you are doing!

CHAPTER 15

THE LAW OF RECIPROCITY

Recipients of gifts (or help) most often feel that they have an obligation to repay those who gave the gift to (or helped) them. An implicit promise exists that if you scratch my back, I'll scratch yours.

To exert influence and build beneficial relationships, you must cultivate and maintain a powerful network of contacts. Think of your network as a mutual assistance alliance in which you give to and help your network partners and in turn, they give to and help you. The object of a network is for people to help one another reach their respective goals. Giving and reciprocating is the glue that holds networks together. Until the debt is paid, the recipient remains obligated to the giver.

Reciprocation is always a tricky issue. It involves questions such as 'how much must you give back?' Societal rules teach us that the repayment should be made in measures that are at least equivalent to the value of that which was received. However, the value of what was received is always a subjective evaluation. It is centered on people's perception.

This estimation of perceived value can be based on a number of aspects, however most people base it primarily on two factors:
  1. How much do you think the gift, help, or favor was worth to the recipient? If the offering was a treasured item

rather than something they were going to throw away, you would have a different perceived obligation to repay them for the gift.

2. What was the perceived cost or burden relative to the giver's overall wealth? For example, if a wealthy person gives you a $100 gift, it would not have the same perceived impact as a person living on a small fixed income giving you the same $100 gift.

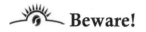 ## Beware!

Shortsighted recipients tend to repay others *at the minimum* of the perceived value of what they received. Those who repay at the low end of the scale are soon regarded as cheapskates who are not truly appreciative. The key to exerting influence via the Law of Reciprocity is to give beyond the minimum; to give generously in order to help others get what they want or need.

Learn to give generously according to the needs and desires of others, not solely on what you want or think you can afford to give. In truth, you can't afford to be cheap because others will shun you. Be generous, make grand gestures, then others will truly extend themselves to help you.

Also, remember that you should never have a 'give to get' attitude. Be liberal in your giving. You will find out soon enough that the world has a wonderful way of rewarding your generosity when you least expect it!

Tsze-Kung asked, "Is there one word which may serve as a rule of practice for all one's life?"

The Master said, "Is not Reciprocity such a word? What you do not want done to yourself, do not do to others."

Confucius

 **THE PROBLEM**

Bob, a corporate Director of Information Services, was stressed out because a project he was heading for the CFO was running behind. Bob's team underestimated the number of man-hours needed for the job; he haphazardly allocated resources and miscalculated his priorities.

Fortunately, Mary, the Director of Human Resources, overheard a conversation between two employees in which one complained, "Bob pulled me off the accounting project to help with a project for the CFO that's in trouble. Now the accounting project's going to be late, too. I don't want to be in trouble with the CFO because his project probably won't be delivered on time. I need two people to help me to even have a chance of getting it done on time, but our head count is completely allocated. Besides, Bob said he couldn't get budget dollars without letting the CFO know that we're in trouble. Now, instead of one project going south, we have two that are doomed!"

STEPS

Step 1: Confront the problem

Although Bob and Mary rarely interacted, she immediately sought him out and told him what she overheard. Bob admitted it was true and confided that he was worried that this disaster would cost him his job. He looked defeated, overwhelmed and at his wit's end.

Step 2: Accept help

Mary asked if she could help. She offered to immediately give Bob two HR employees for a week to handle planning and administrative tasks. She also gave Bob authority to outsource services using funds from her budget, which would cover at least two programmers for the next month. Most importantly, Mary reminded Bob that the troubled program was one that she had initiated and she volunteered to call the CFO that afternoon to suggest changes. Although the changes would delay the implementation date by at least a month, it would provide a better product.

Step 3: Obtain approval for changes

Mary called the CFO who agreed to the changes she suggested.

Step 4: Implement changes

Bob prepared a new plan with new deadlines for the completion of both projects, which he asked Mary to review. Mary reviewed the new plan and told him it looked great. Bob then put the complaining employee back on the CFO's project so it would be completed on time.

☀ THE BOTTOM LINE

Six weeks later, both of the projects were delivered in accordance with the revised time lines. At the end of the year, Bob was promoted and received a large bonus.

As a result of their work together, Bob and Mary became close friends. When Mary's husband was diagnosed with cancer, Bob assigned members of his staff to help Mary's department. He personally cut her lawn each week and Bob's wife weeded Mary's prized rose garden, which was the sanctuary she returned to after spending hours at her husband's bedside. Bob and his son took over Mary's husband's Little League team and took both of Mary's children to every game and practice.

INFLUENCE ILLUSTRATED

The Law of Reciprocity is the driving force behind pork barrel spending in Washington, DC. Politicians understand the Law of Reciprocity -- it's their currency, the capital they exchange. Our representatives know that their initiatives will pass if they agree to support their colleague's pet projects. Right or wrong, it's how our system works.

On a positive note, Habitat for Humanity, the nonprofit organization that builds homes for the underprivileged, utilizes the Law of Reciprocity to help the less fortunate. Prospective homeowners participate in building homes for others before they qualify to have a home built for them. Prospective homeowners log in long, hard hours building other people's homes in order to earn their new home.

Habitat for Humanity is an outgrowth of the traditional Amish barn-building custom. When a member of the Amish community needs a new barn, the entire community – men, women and children – join together to build it in just one day. At the end of that day, a member has a brand-new barn while the others share a sense of enormous pride. They all know that under Amish custom, the favor will be returned -- if not to them, to those they love. In addition, when disasters strike, such as homes burning or being destroyed, Amish communities quickly unite and erect new homes for the unfortunate victims, usually within a week. These wise people know that healing can happen more quickly if the scars of tragedy are erased without delay. They understand that if something similar would happen to their family, they would appreciate a similar act of kindness.

Ideas for Reciprocity

To build a solid foundation of influence use the following reciprocity techniques:

- Link members of your network who can help one another.
- Promptly praise those who achieve success.
- Willingly give referrals to people with whom you currently transact business and to those with whom you wish to do business.
- Send others information they will find useful. Don't send junk mail or spam!
- When a colleague is shorthanded, offer to provide assistance either from yourself or your staff.
- Always express your thanks to those who helped you and promptly return the favor.
- Invite others to join you for breakfast, lunch or business events.
- Fax notes about current business or industry events and developments.
- Congratulate your network partners on their achievements.
- Send cards for special events, birthdays, anniversaries, milestones, etc.

CHAPTER 16

THE LAW OF SATISFACTION & STANDARDS

When we compromise and accept less than what we truly desire, we are seldom fulfilled. Trust your instincts; go with your gut reactions --- only you know what you actually want, how important it is to you to get exactly what you envision, and how you want to achieve your dreams. Remain true to your ideals, maintain your standards, and only then will you be truly satisfied.

Satisfaction revolves around an unwillingness to settle for anything less than your ideal. When you attempt to influence others, determine what they want and deliver it to them as closely to their ideal as possible. If you satisfy them or they think you have the solution to their problem, they will gain confidence in you and stop looking for additional ways to achieve their objective. They will get out of the "seek" mode and your competitors will be out of the running.

What does this mean in business terms? If you solve your clients'/customers' problems so they get exactly what they want, their ideal, they will stop looking for other vendors and buy your product or service. You will become their ideal standard and they will consider you the perfect salesperson to represent them. When your skills match those required to head the project team, you will be the first person asked to lead the group. If a customer believes that your product will be a perfect fit for their needs, you will get the order. It's that simple!

When we settle for less than our ideal, satisfaction may not be forthcoming. Even when we succeed in the eyes of others, fulfillment may be elusive if we don't meet our own standards. Sometimes we are harder on ourselves than we are on others, which can be unnecessarily stressful and unproductive. Check to make sure that your standards are realistic. Monitor your desires and ease any unreasonable standards of perfection. If you don't, it may hold you back.

> Trust yourself. Create the kind of self that you will be happy to live with all your life. Make the most of yourself by fanning the tiny inner sparks of possibility into flames of achievement.
>
> **Foster C. McClellan**

Often, when we take on a project, we are more interested in the process than we are in the outcome. When you become enthralled by the process and lose sight of the end result, you risk compromising your standards. Every small adjustment along the way should be measured against the ideal state. Ask yourself: Will this change make the end result better or worse than what I envisioned? Asking this question frequently is a great way for staying on track with the standards you desire.

In order to influence others, identify their goals and their criteria for reaching those ideal goals. Remember that the ultimate outcome may be secondary to them and responding to the challenge primary. Deliver what they want in a manner that will satisfy them.

 **Beware!**

If, when you perform, the criteria of those who you perform for is compromised, they may not be satisfied with the results you produce. As a result, your ability to influence them will decrease. So perform in accordance with standards that they can embrace.

INFLUENCE ILLUSTRATED

Women always seem to be searching for the "perfect" little black dress, which is sooooo elusive. Finding a black dress isn't difficult, they sell them in most stores, but the "perfect" little black dress always seems to be just out of reach.

Former first lady Jacqueline Kennedy was admired for her elegance, taste, and sense of style. She also seemed to have solved the problem of the perfect little black dress. Reporters noticed that she frequently wore the same outfit and questioned her about it. She explained that the dress was flexible: not too short, not too long, too fancy, or too plain. It could be dressed up or dressed down, worn at the White House for entertaining or elsewhere for social functions. In other words, it was the "perfect" little black dress.

In following up, the reporters asked how long it took Mrs. Kennedy to find the perfect black dress. "Twenty-years," she replied, beaming with great satisfaction. Although to some her quest may have seemed extreme, it made perfect sense to those who refuse to compromise their values.

"Cheshire Cat," she began rather timidly... "Would you tell me, please, which way I ought to go from here?"
"That depends a good deal on where you want to get to," said the cat.

Lewis Carroll [Alice in Wonderland]

 THE PROBLEM

How to get the team leader to understand that you have to deliver what the customer wants according to the customer's standards, not your standards.

In order to please a potentially valuable customer, Mark, a project leader, over-delivered on a contract. The additional items that he provided created delays on the buyer's end and the extra work that his team performed to provide those additional goods and services delayed another important project. I was brought in to help Mark understand why his decisions were counter-productive and costly, and to get him on the right track.

 STEPS

Step 1: Assess the reasons underlying the decision

The project Mark led was for a returning customer that had not placed an order for two years because their last purchase was badly botched. The sales team pressured Mark and told him that the customer, if satisfied, could bring back millions of dollars in business.

Step 2: Compare their standards to the project plan requirements

When I spoke with Mark, he freely admitted that he had added several features and software enhancements that were not on the specs in order to make the customer happy. However, by delivering a more complicated product, it took the project team more time and resources than the project was worth. Mark's company lost money. While the customer felt that the enhancements were great, testing the deliverables took longer than expected. In addition, the extra work that the enhancements required caused another customer's project to fall behind and they were not happy. So, Mark sent two team members to California (at no expense to the customer) to solve the problem.

Step 3: Analyze the cost versus the reward

Mark explained that he made the decision to over-deliver because the customer had expressed doubt about the quality of the company's products and he wanted to win back their business. So, he provided a product that met the standards *he* would have liked if *he* had been the customer. Mark thought the customer would accept a trade-off for any delays that might have been encountered in order to get a better product – especially if the enhancements were free of charge! Unfortunately, Mark's company now had two unhappy customers and the cost of producing the extras ate into the project's profits.

Step 4: Calibrate the hierarchy of standards

Mark used his personal standards – not the customer's requirements – as the measure of what should be delivered. However, he failed to realize that the primary standard for the customer's satisfaction was on-time delivery of exactly what it ordered – nothing more, nothing less.

I asked Mark what he thought would satisfy his boss. He replied that his manager wanted (A) the customer to get what it ordered and be satisfied and (B) the project to show a profit. Mark quickly understood the ramifications of the Law of Satisfaction & Standards. His job was to deliver what the customer and his boss wanted, not what he would have wanted.

I explained to Mark that the key to decision making is to first assess what each party *needs in order to be satisfied*. Then set priorities by determining who must be satisfied.

When I asked Mark how he would prioritize the parties he needed to satisfy, he initially struggled with the answer. "My first inclination was to say 'the customer'. But, my company and my boss have to come first because we have to remain profitable or we won't be around to satisfy the customer in the future. Next, we should try to go the extra mile to give the customer what they want. I must come last! Most of the time, I can balance these priorities and satisfy everyone. I can live with that!" he laughed.

 THE BOTTOM LINE

Mark learned that clearly identifying the precise factors that will satisfy the customer is critical to his corporation's success. He continues to balance the standards and satisfaction requirements of his many stakeholders and teaches his staff to do the same. In the last few years, Mark has been promoted five times. His customer satisfaction numbers are tops in the company and his division is consistently one of the most profitable.

CHAPTER 17

THE LAW OF SCARCITY

Most things are more appealing when they're in short supply. It's the economic principal of supply and demand. People are willing to pay a higher price when items they desire are rare, limited, or not readily available. When the objects of their desires are scarce and/or their window of opportunity is short, people are more apt to take prompt action.

Commodities are usually more valuable when less of them exist or they are less obtainable. Their value generally increases as their availability decreases. Scarcity of time creates a sense of urgency. Auctions --- "Going once, going twice, final offer, last chance. Gone!" --- encourage hesitators to bid. eBay fosters time pressures by prominently listing the days and hours remaining for bids. Coupons with expiration dates, limited time offers, holiday sales and special offerings create time pressures that compel consumers to act with urgency.

Speaking of scarcity, how many packs of cards have kids bought to land the scarcest and most valuable cards? How many adults and children collect rare stamps, coins, sports memorabilia, and limited editions of art, furniture, or antiques? Have you noticed how the price of artwork skyrockets when the artist dies? An artist's death triggers the Law of Scarcity. How many people have bought tickets to "final" or "farewell" concerts?

☀ Beware!

Before you rely on the Law of Scarcity, investigate to determine if the purported scarcity is real or just perceived.

- Is the deadline firm?
- Will the offer actually expire?
- Is only one of the dresses worn by Grace Kelly in *High Society* being sold?
- Has the article been authenticated and, if so, by whom?

Did you know that during production of the film the *Wizard of Oz*, Judy Garland wore many copies of her famous blue and white gingham dress? So when it comes to the Law of Scarcity, get your facts straight and always question whether your actions make good business sense or are emotional responses to perceived scarcity.

My riches consist not in the extent of my possessions but in the fewness of my wants.

J. BROTHERTON

INFLUENCE ILLUSTRATED

King George the First was traveling to Hanover when he stopped for a brief rest in Holland. While waiting for his horses to be readied, he asked for a few eggs. After the eggs were served, he was shocked to learn that he had been charged two hundred florins.

"Eggs must be scarce around this place," the King stated.

"Eggs are plenty enough," the innkeeper replied. "It's kings that are scarce."

King George smiled and paid for the eggs.

THE PROBLEM

How to motivate your employees to perform at their highest levels.

STEPS

Step 1: Reward the top producers

If you have announced a bonus program for your employees, clearly communicate to all that the program was designed to reward special efforts that culminate in superior results. For example, explain that only the top 10% of performers in each department will receive special recognition or bonuses. Invoke scarcity to boost production.

Step 2: Incentive trips

Reward top managers, employees or salespeople with incentive trips. Send them to desirable places, areas they want to visit and will enjoy. I've been to conventions in Florida in August --- that's not a reward; it's a punishment! How can you expect top producers to go the extra mile when you don't clearly demonstrate that you care enough to send them on vacations they can enjoy? If you offer your Northern personnel a shot at a mid-winter trip to sunny Florida, they'll work their tails off to win it. Also, when they get there, give them time to relax and recharge their batteries so that they can post even greater numbers when they return.

Step 3: Give them the limelight

If you want staff members to perform at their best, encourage them to teach others how they excelled at their job. By teaching others, they will tend to work even more effectively. Teaching others usually forces you to examine what you do more carefully. Also, have your personnel lead task forces to create process improvements. Note: Only let the top producers serve; it's a reward and recognition of their outstanding work. The goal is to show other employees that the way to move up in the company is to go the extra mile.

Step 4: Grant top performers status

Select an Employee of the Month, Salesperson of the Year, Manager of the Quarter, and Extra-Miler of the Week. I recommend awarding the Employee of the Month the best parking spot each month. Laminate a sign that announces the Employee of the Month's name and place it prominently so that everyone knows who the extra-milers are.

Step 5: Give rare, unique, or specialized gifts

Award your employees special items they will push hard to win. For example, the opportunity to play golf with a celebrity, receive tickets to a sold out performance, great seats at the Super Bowl, and gift certificates to exclusive spas or salons. Bring in an inspiring motivational speaker to address a small, select audience for a few hours. Arrange for the speaker to have lunch or dinner with your top people or meet with your Employee of the Month. Set up an appointment with the CEO or a company big wig.

THE BOTTOM LINE

Savvy motivators understand that the best people strive to distinguish themselves from the pack. Recognize highly motivated employees and laud them for their efforts, especially for their contributions made while performing in a team environment. Make them feel special and show them you truly value having them as employees. When you demonstrate that you value and appreciate them, they will work even harder to justify and continue receiving your generous thanks.

120

CHAPTER 18

THE LAW OF SIMILARITY AND ATTRACTION

We are more prone to being influenced by others when they share our beliefs, interests, and values. We are also more open to suggestions made by those who have appealing personalities and who look attractive to us. As a rule, we are more comfortable and feel less stress with those who mirror us or who have similar dreams to what we aspire to achieve.

Similarities create bonds, bonds in which people speak the same language, share the same objectives, ideas, aspirations, and values. It's far easier to influence those who share your values and hopes than those who are on a different philosophical, ideological, or cultural wavelength.

Great salespeople instinctively create verbal rapport by finding a degree of commonality, it's the first thing they do. When making new contacts, find connections and interests that you share. When hiring, potential new employees will usually open up when you talk about areas that you have in common.

Search for common ground by asking:

- Does the other person work in your industry?
- Do you know the same people or travel in the similar circles?
- Have you recently seen the same movie?
- Do you have the same likes and dislikes?
- Do you share common hobbies?
- Are your children the same age?
- Do you live in the same area?
- Did you grow up in the same state?
- Did you attend the same college?
- Do you root for the same team or for rivals?
- Have you vacationed in similar venues – do you like the beach or skiing?

Praise, approval and positive reinforcement can increase the bonds of attraction and boost the opportunities to exert influence. It shows people that they are on the right track and that they are performing in a manner that pleases you. Without these guideposts, people often get lost.

Beware!

Offer praise, approval and positive reinforcement ONLY when it's truly deserved. False or unwarranted praise is manipulative and once manipulation is detected, people stop believing you. Resentment, anger and hostility follow. Trust disappears and doors slam tightly closed and become virtually impossible to reopen.

> No man will work for your interests –
> unless they are his.
>
> **David Seabury**

INFLUENCE ILLUSTRATED

During a visit to Vietnam, General William Westmoreland met with a platoon of paratroopers. He asked several of them, "How do you like jumping out of planes?"

"I love it, sir!" the first proudly snapped.

"It's a fantastic experience sir! I couldn't imagine not doing it!" the next loudly sang out.

When Westmoreland asked the third paratrooper, he responded, "I'm scared to death every time, Sir, and don't much like it."

"Then why do you do it?" the General inquired.

"Because I love being around guys who enjoy it," the third paratrooper simply said.

 **THE PROBLEM**

How to connect a manager with a finance background with a sales force? How do you get the sales force to trust the manager, follow his advice, and post the revenue numbers that the CEO demands?

 **STEPS**

Step 1: Assess how the manager used his skills to succeed in the past

Greg, the new VP of Sales & Marketing for a large insurance and investment corporation, had progressively moved up in the corporation by successfully turning around troubled departments. He was viewed by most of the other executives as a young executive on the fast track toward one day becoming a corporate CEO. Greg excelled at cutting costs, eliminating inefficiency, implementing process improvements, holding people accountable, and aligning the right people with the right jobs.

Greg primarily motivated others by using numbers, logical thinking, and legal arguments. He spent his entire career in the home office and had no sales experience. At the home office, he had the power to (1) set the accountability standards, (2) change those standards, and (3) impose consequences for sub-par performance.

Step 2: Define the skills needed for the assignment

When Greg took over, sales were not slipping. In fact, the division was healthy. However, the CEO felt that sales could increase if the agents placed more of their outside business through Greg and his staff. Clearly, influencing skills were critical to get the agents to work through Greg.

Step 3: Determine what worked in the past

The company's insurance and investment sales representatives were semi-independent. They could place as little or as much business with Greg's company as they pleased. As long as they closed a required number of sales to retain their 'agent status', Greg could do little to hold them accountable for placing new business with the corporation. What's more, Greg lacked the authority to change the minimum requirements, and, if he did, the agents would simply take their business elsewhere.

Greg's predecessor, Joseph, was a legend in the industry. He had been a successful salesperson for thirty years before taking over a failing corporate sales office in the Northeast. Within four years, his location became the number one sales office in the entire corporation and remained such until Joseph gave up his office when asked to become an Executive VP at the home office. Salespeople loved him! He was one of them. The top sales producers gushed when they spoke about Joseph, but they said that Greg simply "cruised in," showed them a bunch of meaningless charts filled with numbers and projections, and didn't even have the time (or sense) to stay for lunch.

A million-dollar producer had phoned Greg's office to invite him for lunch or dinner to meet several top salespeople. In response to the invitation, Greg's assistants replied, "He couldn't possibly do that because he has email to attend to in the evening and another flight to catch to the next city – he is SOOO BUSY!" Her partner added that, "Joseph would have understood that relationships bring in business. Greg doesn't even know that our business is about people – not charts. He can post all the numbers he wants, but we don't have to give him a dime of our business – we don't need him – he needs US."

Step 4: Identify problems and set out a strategy

I reviewed my findings with Greg and together we laid out a strategy.

We began by identifying the problem. First, Greg was following in the footsteps of a well-loved, highly respected legend, who was a tough act to follow. Second, Greg never sold anything. And he readily admitted that he didn't know how to sell as well as the people he was charged with leading.

Our strategy was to:
- Bring Joseph back as a consultant to make Greg's transition smoother. Have Joseph alert Greg to areas of commonality he had with top producers from which Greg could start to build relationships.

- Arrange for Joseph and Greg to talk on a regular basis and continue to have Joseph share his knowledge with Greg. I put together a "fact and interest database" for Greg to compile. In it, he recorded information about the agents' likes and dislikes and, most important, areas that he and the agents had in common. For example, Greg's brother died at a young age from leukemia and I knew that two agents supported the Make a Wish Foundation. I instructed Greg's assistant to contact the agents to ask when their next fundraising event was scheduled so that Greg could attend and lend financial support. With the assistance of Joseph, and others in the company, we compiled a substantial database focused on the agents' interests, families, and business needs so that Greg can establish a degree of commonality with them quickly. It refreshes his memory about people's interests and helps him to find out current information about them. To this day, Greg insists that it gets updated frequently. He told me this database is invaluable and has contributed substantially to his success. Greg still references it whenever he visits remote offices, when he chats to people by telephone, or prior to responding to email requests.

- Formulate a strategy to counter-balance the lack-of-sales argument. We formed an agent's committee that focused on information technology improvements and customer service innovations. Greg and the head of the agent's advisory council were the co-chairs. From this platform, Greg became the agents' champion. His theme was that his job was to make their job easier.

- Align Greg with the excellence of the top salespeople. We put together an audio series and distributed one tape each month to the agents for a year. We brought the corporation's top producers from all over the country into a studio to tape their best, most productive sales ideas and Greg interviewed them. Even though he wasn't a sales expert, Greg was soon perceived as the provider of innovative and profitable sales ideas.

THE BOTTOM LINE

After a rocky start, Greg regrouped and began building relationships with the producers. Although Greg realized the sales people knew that he did not have direct selling experience in the field, the sales force quickly understood that his job was convincing them that he was in many ways similar. His job didn't involve selling directly to the company's customers. Greg's primary focus was 'internal sales'. He was constantly selling the agent's ideas and needs to upper level management and the Board. And to the agents' surprise, they found that Greg was better at getting them what they needed than Joseph had been!

Greg successfully championed the agents' causes because he had been groomed in the home office. The home office personnel responded to Greg's style because it was similar to theirs and they were comfortable with it. Greg was more influential in that environment than Joseph, who despite all his success was considered a sales guy, not a 'home office guy'. However, Joseph's field skills were invaluable to Greg, who said that he learned more in three months just from watching Joseph interact and build rapport with the sales force than he could have in twenty years on his own.

CHAPTER 19

THE LAW OF SOCIETAL PRESSURE

Our community is usually the rudder of our ship; we look to its values for our direction. When making decisions, we follow the ethics and guidelines of our society, community, and culture for support and direction. To be accepted, we play according to the ground rules that govern our society. The people with whom we interact on a regular basis strongly influence our actions, decisions, and behavior.

As humans we are influenced by the way others think, feel, and act. We look to them to learn the rules, to measure where we stand, and to decide what we should do. Societal norms --- rules on what is right or wrong --- frame how we perceive situations, memories, or events. They influence what we recall, the significance we attach to what happens to us, and help shape how we should act.

When questions arise, we observe others. We ask people in our circle their opinions to determine what is proper and correct. And we tend to act in accordance with the behavior of those we respect instead of going against it.

We get stuck in our ways. We form patterns, routines, and formulaic behavior. Often, we are deaf to input from others and blind to change because we march to the beat of societal norms. According to behavioral studies, when presented with facts that conflict with our beliefs, we tend to reject newly introduced facts.

As creatures of habit, we store and catalogue information according to what is least stressful and most comfortable. Stress and discomfort result from not adhering to social norms, from being --- or fearing that you will become --- an outsider. When we try to process information that runs contrary to societal norms, our comfort level usually plunges and our stress level soars.

⛯ Beware!

Societal norms constantly change; and so should you. Much of today's accepted behavior and communication was considered shocking, rude, and uncouth in the 1900's. The problem arises when we formulate ideas, beliefs, and decisions solely on the basis of information that makes the most sense to us now. Frequently, that information reflects only your past experiences and knowledge basis. Understand that when you make judgments that affect the future, they are based on your current beliefs and societal norms, which soon may be out of date. The result is often unwarranted prejudice.

So, think twice before you reject ideas and suggestions that don't conform to your current beliefs. *Try to imagine tomorrow – you might not think the same way.* By remembering this simple philosophy – I find that I am better at keeping my mind open to new ideas and suggestions.

People look to you and me to see what they are supposed to be. And, if we don't disappoint them, maybe, just maybe, they won't disappoint us.

Walt Disney

INFLUENCE ILLUSTRATED

Former President Calvin Coolidge invited friends from Vermont to dine at the White House. Concerned that they might unintentionally act inappropriately, Coolidge's friends decided to mimic the President's actions to be sure that they acted correctly.

The dinner went smoothly until coffee was served. Then, Coolidge poured some of his coffee into his saucer and his guests did the same. He added sugar, cream and stirred and his guests followed suit. Then Coolidge reached down and gave the saucer to his cat.

 THE PROBLEM

How to establish societal norms for your workgroup that will provide the standards you expect your people to meet and will help you manage them effectively and efficiently.

☀ STEPS

Step 1: Establish a Team Commitment Contract [1]

A team commitment contract is an agreement in which all team members participate in setting the team's standards and expectations. By involving team members in the establishment of the societal rules, peer pressure is exerted in a positive manner. Members' involvement also helps to assure the setting of realistic, achievable standards that are based on the practical know-how of the members.

Step 2: Explain the team commitment contract

Fully explain the team commitment contract so that all team members understand it, their roles and the roles of other team members. Inform each member how his/her contribution relates to the overall project or company objectives. Evaluate the group's societal norms throughout the project. Frequently repeat each member's roles during the project.

Step 3: Obtain all team members' agreement

Enlist the assistance of the team members in getting all members to agree to the team commitment contract. Unanimous agreement will make managing the group easier because groups that agree to the expectations and standards

---

[1] Described in detail in the Indaba Teambuilding manual

that they set, effectively self-manage themselves. This makes any remaining managerial tasks less stressful and time-consuming and provides time for other focuses.

Step 4: Praise and acknowledge

Clearly compliment and publicly commend outstanding efforts and achievements. Encourage group members to praise, acknowledge and thank other group members on their accomplishments.

Step 5: Noncompliance

If a team member fails to adhere to the established societal norms, first the team and especially the affected members should be encouraged to apply pressure until the wayward member falls into line. Usually, an affected member will complain to the group that he/she is not meeting his/her goals because of the other member's delinquent behavior.

Step 6: New members

When a new member enters the group, clearly explain the standards and his/her role. Instruct the new member to look to other team members for examples of how to act and have existing team members mentor the new member. Periodically, reiterate the team standards and go over the team commitment contract.

☀ THE BOTTOM LINE

The essential goal of a team commitment contract is to set and record the standards on how the team should function. Give all team members a copy of the commitment contract, which will reduce misunderstandings and prevent many problems.

In creating a team commitment contract, four elements must always be considered.

The Four Elements of the Team Commitment Contract are:

Safety – Both from a (1) psychological and (2) physiological standpoint.

(1) *Psychological*: To perform well, team members must feel that their jobs are secure. They must know that team members will support their efforts and that team meetings are open forums where members can voice their opinions without fear.

(2) *Physiological*: Team members must also be confident that if they work late, the building will be safe, and that they can exit the building and travel home without fear. In addition, they should feel assured that you have provided safe tools and work areas.

Support – let all team members know they can count on the organization and on the team. Always foster a supportive environment.

Education - Growth & Learning – When people learn, they are both motivated and challenged. When boredom sets in, complacency quickly follows.

Fun - Enjoyment & Satisfaction – Employees want to get up in the morning and look forward to going to work, not dreading another day. Happy workers are more productive and tend not to switch companies frequently. Discuss with your people what makes them happy. Remember to inject some fun into your team.

133

CHAPTER 20

THE LAW OF STATUS

People give greater respect to and have more faith in the words and beliefs of those who have prestige, power and esteemed reputations. The greater one's status or importance, the greater the influence he/she will be able to exercise.

Build the strongest possible reputation. Guard it well and others will compete for your counsel. In most societies, status and power go hand-in-hand; they are inseparable. The higher you ascend in your arena, the more others will seek your wisdom.

Status is granted because of our perception of a person's:

- Power and authority
- Knowledge or expertise
- Wealth and position
- Family and community ties
- Public image or political clout
- Celebrity
- Religious or charitable affiliations and/or deeds
- Uniqueness
- Beauty, attractiveness and/or physical strength

When you are considered to be an important person, others will usually comply with your requests and defer to you. When you have status, the reach of your influence will extend to a wider range of people. When you have status, others will listen, be courteous and often follow simply because of your status.

How do you combat the situation in which others believe that their status and authority outweighs yours? Simply by elevating yours! To wield power and influence, raise your status so that it is at least equal, but preferably above, theirs.

Improve your status by staying calm and remaining in control. Losing your temper, displaying irritation, anger or negative emotions will show that you are not always in control. It will frighten and/or anger others, who may then choose to avoid you. All of this will lower your status and decrease your influence.

Beware!

As a manager, you have the fiduciary responsibility to make certain that you eliminate opportunities that your staff may have to abuse their status. One Napoleon could sink your entire kingdom... especially if that person alienates your valuable customers or employees! Take great efforts to ensure that your personnel clearly understand that misuse of their status will not be tolerated.

Getting anything changes it from being desirable to just taken for granted.

UNKNOWN

INFLUENCE ILLUSTRATED

The day after his Secretary of Labor resigned, President Woodrow Wilson was approached by a White House maid who asked him to consider her husband for the vacancy. Her husband, she explained, was perfect for the position because, "He was a laboring man, who knew what labor was, and understood laboring people."

Wilson told her that he appreciated her recommendation and added that serving as Secretary of Labor was an important position "that required an influential person."

"But if you made him the Secretary of Labor, my husband WOULD be an influential person!" the maid promptly replied.

THE PROBLEM

How to reach your objectives in the face of an entrenched, unyielding bureaucracy.

In Pennsylvania, we have been hounded to sign up for the EZ Pass System for toll roads. I did and I've been thrilled because it's quick, easy, monitors your entering and exiting and charges your account appropriately. In the areas I travel, you can use any toll lane whether it is marked for EZ Pass access or not.

Shortly before this book went to press, I exited the Pennsylvania Turnpike at the Morgantown interchange. It was rush hour and thinking that all booths were EZ Pass equipped, I went through the closest tollbooth, which did not take EZ Pass.

As I drove through, the green light did not flash, so I looked in my rear view mirror and saw the toll collector waving at me. I backed up and he told me that my lane was not EZ Pass compatible. He instructed me to drive in reverse through the tollbooth, cross several lanes of oncoming rush hour traffic and exit through an EZ Pass lane.

I attempted to back up, but cars were entering my lane. The toll collector did not help by stopping oncoming cars, he simply watched. Since backing up was so unsafe, I explained my fears to the collector. I asked him to wave my EZ pass device under the tollbooth so it would register and bill me electronically. He stated that was impossible because the sensor had to calculate my car's weight to bill me appropriately.

I asked if there was another solution and he told me that I could pay the toll for the entire road, which was $11.25. I was in trouble! Because I was only picking up a package, I had left my purse in the office. I only had about $5.00 in charge in the car. I told him about my cash problem and added that I thought that

137

was unfair to pay that much because my actual toll was only fifty cents. He said since I couldn't prove it, I would have to pay the full toll. I suggested several ways that I could 'prove it'. He refused to call the interchange where I entered to verify my claim or to call my office, on my cell phone, to confirm the time I left. Calling, he said, would prove nothing and "rules were rules."

Since I didn't have enough cash to pay the full amount, I asked if my toll could be deducted from my EZ Pass account or could I send a check? He agreed that I could pay by mail and I exclaimed, "Great that solves everything, you can just bill me." The collector then asked for my license, wrote down my information and went back to his tollbooth. I assumed everything was fine and off I drove.

Shortly after I arrived at my office, a state trooper telephoned and told me that the toll collector issued a complaint charging me with a violation. I was stunned! I told the trooper my story, but he said that the collector claimed that I had evaded the toll after stopping and that I simply drove off without paying or signing the necessary paperwork. I asked the officer to have the toll collector put the papers in the mail; then I would sign them and send a check. "No. They insist you drive back to Morgantown and pay the fine in cash within the next two hours or you will have to go to traffic court," he announced.

Even though he said he believed me and agreed that the Turnpike should be more accommodating, the trooper stated that if I didn't return to the Morgantown exit, he would be forced to issue a citation that carried a $200 fine *plus* a court appearance *plus* a moving ticket violation would be attached to my driver's license information. I explained that the trip would take more than two hours, that I had to pick up my two young children and didn't want to take them to Morgantown since a winter storm was coming in. In fact, it had already started snowing. I asked the trooper to call the Turnpike supervisor to ask if I could send a check by mail, pay by credit card, or have the money taken from my EZ Pass account.

Within ten minutes, the state trooper called back. He said that the Morgantown personnel insisted that I return to Morgantown within two hours or face a court appearance. He apologized profusely and told me he was sorry for the inconvenience.

I arranged for my children to be taken home and drove to the Morgantown interchange. I was kept waiting for an hour without being allowed to pay the $11.25. So, I decided to speak to the supervisor. I asked how often this problem occurs and she informed me, "This happens to at least half a dozen people a day!" The supervisor explained that the system cannot adjust when drivers go through non-EZ Pass lanes and regretted that she lacked the authority to let me pay by mail. She also volunteered that she had repeatedly asked her manager to address the problem.

 **STEPS**

Step 1: Call those responsible for change

The following day I called my State Senator, EZ Pass management, and Turnpike management. None responded, which is precisely what I expected. I realized that they considered me some ordinary citizen with little status or clout who was not worthy of a response.

Step 2: Haul out the heavy artillery

After six days without a response, I told a politically connected friend that neither my State Senator nor anyone from his office, EZ Pass officials, or the Pennsylvania Turnpike Commission had returned my call. I asked him to give my biography to those who could help fix the problem. I made it clear that the system was broken and should be fixed so others would not have to go through the same horror.

Step 3: Get your story told

That same day, I called another friend who works for one of Philadelphia's most widely listened to talk-radio stations. The station gave me ten minutes of airtime to tell my story.

Step 4: Spread the word

I called my political friend again and told him them to tune in to the talk station at 5:30 PM --- smack dab in the middle of the rush-hour drive time when a wide audience listens. I also called the State Trooper and left a message for him to listen. On a roll, I left messages for the Morgantown supervisor, the manager of the EZ Pass system, and several Turnpike managers.

THE BOTTOM LINE

My story played well. Callers voiced their outrage at the Turnpike Official's abuse of power and lack of customer service. The station was swamped with calls from others who had been abused by IRS clerks, Postal Service workers, toll collectors, government customer service representatives, and other rule keepers who think that their positions and status entitle them to make our lives miserable.

Let me be clear that 99 percent of those who enforce the rules do not abuse their power. However, one percent does and that's way too much because these few can cause major, unnecessary and unfair problems.

Has the problem been fixed? Not as we go to press, but I know they're working on it because every two days someone calls me with an update. I know from the responses that the system will be changed and changed soon.

Had I had not invoked the Law of Status would change be imminent? Absolutely not! Action is now being taken simply because I got the word out loud and clear, which substantially elevated my status with the Pennsylvania Turnpike Authority.

CHAPTER 21

THE LAW OF 3RD PARTY ENDORSEMENT

Many people are influenced to take action when those they respect and admire endorse certain positions. It's why famous movie stars are used as spokespersons for products. As a result of endorsements, people buy products and services, change their beliefs and otherwise involve themselves. Endorsements provide support for their decisions. People take comfort in knowing that they are not the first to be convinced.

Whenever you successfully complete a project, get endorsements or testimonials from those you helped. When you have endorsements from satisfied clients and/or customers in hand, you will have a much better chance of selling yourself to others.

Endorsements and testimonials build influence. They give you more credibility, especially when the commendations come from people who others respect and admire. The greater the endorser's renown and reputation, the greater weight his/her testimonial carries.

 Beware!

We assume that powerful people would not lend their names to endorse items that they don't believe in, but they often have ulterior motives. They may have been paid handsomely for voicing their support. Endorsers may have a stake or ownership interest in the product, cause, or service, or they may simply be helping a friend, relative, or returning a favor. Unscrupulous promoters can fabricate endorsements. Deceitful people know that most people will never bother to look below the surface. Are you letting yourself be unduly influenced by a 3rd party endorsement that you have not checked out? Trusting people rarely check until it is too late. So beware – determine the reasons underlying all 3rd party endorsements and find out if they are genuine. And while you're at it, check yourself. Are you perhaps giving an endorsement more weight than it deserves just because a powerful person sanctioned the product or service?

Character is like a tree and reputation like its shadow. The shadow is what we think of it; the tree is the real thing.

Abraham Lincoln (1809 - 1865), Lincoln's Own Stories

INFLUENCE ILLUSTRATED

As the first black major-league baseball player, Jackie Robinson was prepared to receive abuse from fans as well as his fellow baseball players. Players called him hateful names and physically assaulted him by deliberately going out of their way to run into and over him. Crowds taunted him with demeaning racial slurs, jeers and insults.

In midseason of 1947, Robinson was having a bad game in both the field and at the plate. The crowd was relentless and responded to each of his mistakes with prolonged booing and cruel, hurtful words.

On the field, Pee Wee Reese --- the Dodgers' shortstop, captain and most respected player, who also was a Southerner --- walked over to Robinson between first and second base. In front of the vicious crowd, Reese put his arm around Robinson and stood nobly. His act was an embrace that signified to everyone in the ballpark, to everyone in baseball, his acceptance of the black baseball player and his complete and total solidarity with his teammate.

Subsequently, Robinson declared, "That gesture saved my career. Pee Wee made me feel as if I belonged."

Reese's endorsement of Robinson encouraged others to more readily accept Robinson, who went on to have an outstanding career.

3ʀᴅ PARTY ENDORSEMENT AND LEADERSHIP

 THE PROBLEM

How to overcome resistance to the implementation of a process improvement program at a multinational corporation.

For three years, the company spent millions of dollars developing the program and sent wave after wave of managers and employees through training, but the implementation of the program was floundering. Although the managers seemed to believe in the fundamental principles of the program, they continually ignored the program changes, reverted to their old ways, and did not reward workers who were utilizing new processes explained in class. Those charged with implementing the program were sabotaged. They were excluded from meetings, their efforts were thwarted, and mean-spirited jokes proliferated about those who had been trained to execute the new system.

STEPS

Step 1: Identify the problem

I met with Claudia, who had been placed in charge of the program and directed to make it operational. The biggest hurdle, she explained, was that those who championed the program felt that their careers could be ruined if their names were associated with it. She couldn't convince influence-makers to openly announce their support for the implementation of the new program.

144

Step 2: Identify the players

After placing the organizational chart on the table, I asked Claudia:
1. Who brought the program to the corporation?
2. Who, at the highest level, would be held accountable if the program failed?
3. Who would be in line for a bonus or promotion if the program succeeded?"

Step 3: Ascertain who could endorse the program

The prior CEO had started the program, but Claudia did not know what impact his involvement would have on the current CEO. We decided not to approach the current CEO to discuss the problem because he was so new to the job. We also didn't want his first impression of Claudia to be that she was struggling with her assignment to get the program up and running.

At his last company, the CEO had great success implementing this program. I heard him speak and remembered that he stressed how valuable the initiative had been in changing how his old company operated. I also knew that a tape of the speech existed and hoped that it was still available. I suggested to Claudia that she contact the CEO's assistant to see if she had the tape on file and to explain why she wanted it. Two days later, we had the tape and the CEO's assistant had secured his permission for us to use the clip pertaining to the program. I sent flowers to her on the spot!

Step 4: Assign accountability at the proper level

Implementation of the program was in limbo because the senior executive in charge had been reassigned and would be going overseas within the month. Fortunately, Claudia was friendly with him and he was on excellent terms with the CEO. She knew that no decision had been made on who would replace him. She knew he was aware that we needed a powerful champion in the organization – someone who people would listen to and follow. Without an influential supporter, the program was doomed.

I asked Claudia to set up a brainstorming meeting with the outgoing executive. I recommended that she leverage his help by stating that he could ensure his legacy by giving responsibility for the program's implementation to a powerful successor. I suggested that adding a powerful successor would help to establish the program and protect the outgoing executive from blame if the program failed.

Step 5: Stress the rewards for endorsers

We needed managers at all levels and at every location to endorse the benefits that would be derived from implementing the program. Specifically, we asked them for letters and audiovisual testimonials unequivocally declaring how imperative it was for all employees to apply the information they had learned in the training sessions. We informed potential endorsers that to promote the implementation of the program, we were putting together an information and marketing package. The format of the package would center on the CEO's supportive comments and be uploaded onto the corporate website. The best endorsements from mangers, Claudia explained, would also be included in the package.

Step 6: Be selective in choosing endorsers

We drew up a list of those whose endorsements we believed would carry the most weight and then invited them to view the clip containing the CEO's endorsement. We asked if they would like to appear in the video in the package or provide a written statement on their view of the importance of the program to the corporation.

Claudia was quickly inundated with requests to participate from managers who wanted to make sure the right people knew that they endorsed the program. We gave most of the airtime to those who had already implemented the process and who had achieved good results. Proof that the program was working started pouring in. Those who couldn't yet provide us with good results put pressure on their people to get results. It was fascinating and beautiful to watch! Claudia and her new boss were overjoyed by the response.

 # THE BOTTOM LINE

Within three weeks, over two hundred of the company's most influential people competed to be included in the marketing package. Such a response would not have been possible without making them aware of the CEO's comments. His powerful endorsement of the program secured the support of numerous influential figures throughout the company. The buzz we created convinced a new and powerful senior executive to sign on to lead the initiative. After viewing the CEO's clip, he realized how important the program was to his new boss so he agreed to take the program under his wing.

In the first twelve months, implementation of the program was widely embraced throughout the corporation. In fact, Claudia's results were 60% higher than target, an astonishing success considering the initial resistance she faced. It was a clear tribute to the power of endorsements.

As a result of her success, Claudia was asked to head the Internal Communications and Training Department even though she had no prior experience in the area. It was a substantial and unexpected promotion. As we go to press, Claudia is excelling at her new job and will never forget the power of 3rd Party Endorsements.

ABOUT INDABA: THE COMPANY

We believe in accountability.
We achieve long-term results.

Organizations are more challenged than ever. Competition is greater. Customers' expectations are higher. Technology is advancing at the speed of light. The bar continues to rise at a resounding rate. Employees and organizations need to align properly to maximize cooperation among employees.

Clients look to us because we consistently solve problems and implement solutions.

Indaba Motivation & Education

What is Indaba recognized for? Indaba's primary focus has always been to provide seminars that positively enhance profitability. We educate employees in solid business principles, processes and practices so that they understand how to make decisions that add to their company's bottom line. The fundamental basis for Indaba presentations are advanced techniques for communication, behavior modification, and management and employee development. Programs revolve around the psycho-dynamics of peak performance. The processes taught involve:
➢ Building advanced communication models
➢ Improving and analyzing current competencies
➢ Learning and implementing new skills, and
➢ Providing the impetus for behavior modification.

What makes our organization unique?

- We have designed creative and customized training courses for optimum learning and employee development. These can be delivered by Indaba trainers or by your training department.
- We teach advanced psychological models with the goal of behavior modification.
- Indaba has a proven track record of success since 1988.
- We have an extensive network of experienced trainers, coaches and consultants.

148

- We have worked with a range of industries and many diverse organizations

Indaba Training Specialists, Inc. focuses on training, consulting, and improving individual and organizational effectiveness.
We specialize in:

- Teamwork
- Leadership Development
- Change
- Influence & Communication
- Delivering Feedback and Receiving Coaching
- Advanced Communication Skills
- Sales and Negotiation
- Executive Coaching
- Customer Service
- RA² Interface – Responsibility, Accountability, and Authority
- Customized Executive and Team Retreats

Corporate leaders find that they benefit from having us come in to provide an objective view. We can help you grow people and develop strong leaders. Indaba consultants have established a track record of success with executives, teams, managers and employees to implement behavioral modification and change. Indaba assists you in reaching goals and quickly creating organizational alignment based on accountability and profitability. How? Our certified consultants and instructors teach psychological models of excellence and we help you put them into action within your company.

Partial Client Partnership list:

Air Products, Allegheny Power, American College of Physicians, Allstate Insurance, Ardmore Alliance, AT&T, Blue Cross Blue Shield of NJ, Businessman's Life of Kansas, Centra Financial Group, CoreStates Bank, Corum Healthcare, DVFG Financial Group, Eastwood Company, E.F Hutton, First Capital Holdings, GE Medical, GMAC, Hansch Financial Group, Icon Clinical Research, Leadership Peak, Lee Hecht Harrison, Liberty Life, Lincoln Financial Planning, Lutheran Brotherhood, Massachusetts Mutual Life, Meridian Bank, MetraHealth, Metropolitan Life, MISO, National Computer Services, National Association of Female Executives, Nationwide Provident, NE ISO, North West Mutual, Pacific Corinthian, Parke-Davis Pharmaceutical, PECO Energy, PennDot, Pfizer Pharmaceutical, Philadelphia 76ers, PJM Interconnection, Prism, Provident Mutual, Prudential Life, Raytheon, Sears Financial Corporation, ShopRite Supermarkets, Southwest Power Pool, Spohn Medical, St. Paul Companies, State Farm Insurance, Sun Corporation, Texas A&M, Ursinus College, U.S. Senators, Verizon, Wakefern Corporation, Warner-Lambert Pharmaceuticals, Wharton School of Business

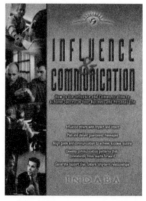

The 21 Laws of Influence

The 21 Laws of Influence will help you to clearly understand how people are persuaded and how others affect our beliefs. The course provides the basis for deciding which strategies will be most effective on those you must influence and will educate people to avoid getting caught in a web of influence or roped into a persuasive argument without being aware of the mechanics of persuasion.

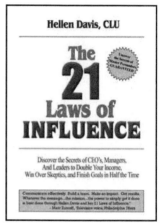

ISBN: 1-58570-072-X
8.5 x 11 hardcover
160 pages
Price: $19.95

Influence & Communication

This book provides the means to break the communication code wide open. Just imagine if you had the power to understand the exact meaning and intent of communication. Picture being able to decode messages you receive. What if you could transmit the exact meanings necessary to achieve your goals? What potential!

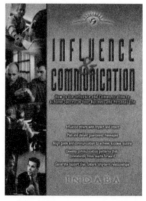

ISBN: 1-58570-101-7
8.5 x 11 paperback
202 pages
Price: $29.95

150

Alignment: -- The RA² Interface

Have you restructured, downsized, upsized, matrixed, aligned functionally, streamlined systematically, but haven't had the results you expected?

Have you found it challenging to simultaneously stay on track, accelerate change, sustained momentum, create the future, do everything faster and still motivate employees?

Are you looking for organizational answers that meet today's market demands and employee needs?

Alignment - RA² Interface will help you marry expectations and metrics –

Deploy people with:

1. Clearly defined responsibility.
2. Accountability - benchmark metrics as previously agreed upon
3. Authority factors necessary to complete goals. The goal is to foster intercompany and intradepartmental cooperation and alignment.

ISBN: 1-58570-160-2
8.5 x 11 paperback
202 pages
Price: $29.95

How to Deliver Feedback & Receive Coaching

How do you grow employees if you don't deliver feedback effectively? This course provides the processes on how a manager should deliver feedback objectively with a focus on growing the employee, and from the employee's standpoint - - how to receive feedback with an open mind.

ISBN: 1-58570-291-9
8.5 x 11 paperback
124 pages
Price: $29.95

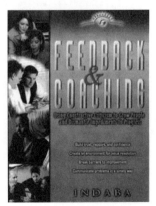

Teambuilding

Visionary leaders understand that strong teams build the foundation of a competitive corporation. Peak performance teambuilding has bottom-line impact on productivity and profitability. This book teaches comprehensive team-based accelerated-learning strategies.

The teambuilding models in this book will help dynamically change individual and team behavior. These innovative ideas will assist with the development and implementation of a game plan focused on team-based results. The models and techniques create powerful leverage points to build peak performance teams. These are used to put team strategies into action to enhance productivity, motivation and profits.

ISBN: 1-58570-383-4
8.5 x 11 paperback
120 pages
Price: $29.95

Change -- Is Your Organization on Fire?

Employees are taught to deal effectively with the phases of change. The goal is to move your people through change in a manner that stokes creativity and innovation, enhancing corporate goals and visions.

ISBN: 1-58570-307-9
8.5 x 11 paperback
202 pages
Price: $29.95

Sales and Marketing - Leap to the Next Level

Targeted behavioral changes build superior salespeople. This MBA-like course is specifically designed to drive individuals to reach the next level of sales and best influence customers with their personal style. The goal is to establish long-term client relationships and increase product and service purchases.

Call for information on this customized program

INDABA

For more information on Train-the-Trainer programs, consultant programs and training materials, bulk pricing on products, and speaker information please contact our office.

(610) 993-8047

Power point presentations, manuals and audio materials are available through our website.

www.Indaba1.com

For information on this book please go to www.21laws.com

ABOUT THE AUTHOR

Hellen C. Davis, CLU

- Executive coach
- Corporate strategist
- Self-made millionaire
- Entrepreneur
- Motivational keynote speaker

Hellen Davis has accumulated over two decades of sales and management experience and is currently the President and CEO of Indaba Training Specialists, Inc. Her strengths are the ability to assist clients in influencing their employees and clients. Ms. Davis has an excellent track record in strategic planning, behavior modification, sales and peak performance proficiencies. Indaba, with her leadership, has produced numerous audio cassette series, corporate manuals, support and training materials and workbooks; including several based on the cutting edge techniques in the field of Neurolinguistics -- specifically designed for sales, marketing, customer service and management professionals.

Over the past two decades, Hellen has delivered motivational, strategic planning and sales presentations worldwide. She lived overseas in Africa and Europe for more than twenty years and shares her global philosophy with audiences.

"**Philadelphia Magazine**" voted Hellen Davis as one of Philadelphia's "*Women to Watch*" because of her business acumen, her contributions to the area's networking affiliates and women's business organizations, her role in raising consciousness for effective networking and her good standing in the community. She resides in the Philadelphia area with her husband, Jack, and their two children, Jazmin and Justin.

Hellen has graced the cover of "**Main Line Today**" magazine, headlining an article entitled, "*Women in Charge*" and is quoted in numerous national and regional publications and newspapers. Ms. Davis has been a guest on many talk shows and has appeared on a large variety of TV and radio stations across the country including CNN, Dateline, and EXTRA.

Hellen Davis has had more than twenty years of experience in management & consulting. She is well respected for her extensive knowledge of behavioral modification processes, communication & management development, sales management practices and training techniques, and negotiation tactics. Hellen Davis has an impressive knowledge of the international marketplace. She is fluent in several languages. She founded, owned and operated an import/export company in South Africa dealing with Europe, the Far East, and other African countries, the United States and Canada. She is also currently on the Board of Directors of 30glycolic.com, which supplies goods online throughout North America, Europe, Asia and Africa.

Hellen Davis is Past President of the Main Line Women's Network, past President of Women's Capital Funding, a past Board Member of The Women's Referral Network of Chester County, Past President of the Tri-County Business Alliance, current Board Member of the YMCA Heritage Foundation, and a Charter Member of the National Association of Female Executives.

Availability: Philadelphia, PA, New Jersey, New York, Delaware, Washington, DC, nationwide by arrangement and via telephone; flexible and often available for last minute interviews.

Indaba (610) 993-8047
Indaba1.com   21laws.com